THE RIVER PLATE REPUBLICS

A Survey of
The Religious, Economic and Social
Conditions in

Argentina, Paraguay and Uruguay

By
WEBSTER E. BROWNING
Ph.D., F.R.G.S.

*Executive Secretary of the Committee on Co-operation,
Buenos Aires, Argentine*

WORLD DOMINION PRESS
1, Tudor Street, London, E.C. 4
113, Fulton Street, New York City

1928

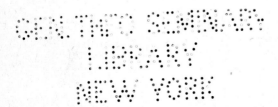

PRINTED BY
WILSON'S PRINTING COMPANY, LTD.,
67b, TURNMILL STREET,
LONDON, E.C. I.

Printed in Great Britain.

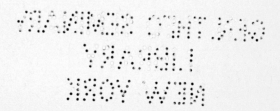

FOREWORD

THE WORLD DOMINION SURVEY SERIES attempts to describe briefly and clearly the situation in the various countries of the world as viewed from the standpoint of the Kingdom of God.

We are glad to be able to present to the Christian Church another contribution to the survey of Latin America.

Dr. Browning is well qualified to give a complete view of the situation in the River Plate Republics, where he is Secretary of the Committee on Co-operation. We are much indebted to the Rev. T. S. Donohugh, of the Methodist Episcopal Church, Secretary for South America, for going through the page proof and making a number of useful suggestions.

This volume is a ringing challenge. "Unless mighty efforts are now made to save the country, it will degenerate into a godless and atheistic land." None who render supreme loyalty to the Lord Jesus Christ can read such words unmoved.

But there is much to encourage, and in spite of the Argentine Educator who is quoted by Dr. Browning as saying "I do not believe in the efficacy of the Bible for modern mentality," a quiet deep work is being done among the poor in spirit, and such as hunger for God. The Bible has been used, apart from the instrumentality of any preacher, in innumerable cases to bring light into dark hearts and homes, and Churches can be counted by hundreds throughout the continent, that owe their origin to the reading of a portion of Scripture sold by a passing colporteur.

ALEXANDER McLEISH,

Survey Editor.

November, 1928.

PREFACE

THIS Survey is an attempt to describe in the briefest outline possible, within certain pre-scribed limits, the social, economic and especially the religious, conditions which prevail in what are generally known abroad as the " River Plate Republics." These are Argentina, Paraguay and Uruguay, the three countries that border the muddy waters of the Rio de la Plata and its great tributaries of the interior.

Although the conditions which prevail in this territory are akin to similar conditions in neighbouring areas, and the problems that confront the evangelical forces are common to the Latin Republics of the Western Hemisphere, the author has confined himself to describing the situation prevailing in the area under consideration.

It has been impossible to secure absolute exactness in the statistics given, due not only to the multiplicity of the religious groups, but also to reticence on the part of some of the smaller societies in giving information regarding their work. The official representatives of the larger organizations have been generous in giving help, and the thanks of the writer are hereby accorded them.

In justice to the work it must also be stated that the errors of omission, if any, since they affect only a few of the smallest groups, do not greatly change the final results, and certainly do not invalidate the conclusions as a whole. By means of careful criticism by interested and competent friends, approximate exactness has been secured, probably as nearly complete as it is possible to obtain in any similar work.

For a fuller discussion of many points which have only been touched upon in our limited space, the interested reader is referred to the two volumes which constitute the Report of the " Congress on Christian Work in South America," held in Montevideo, March to April, 1925. These volumes may be obtained from the publishers, the Fleming H. Revell Company, 156, Fifth Avenue, New York, or from the Committee on Co-operation in Latin America, 419, Fourth Avenue, New York City. The author's own volumes, *Roman Christianity in Latin America* and *New Days in Latin America*, would also be helpful in giving a wider view of the field and its problems, and can be secured through the Committee named above.

In the present work, as in all his writings, the author has endeavoured to preserve a conciliatory attitude and to give due credit to existing values. Reference to the Roman Catholic Church has been necessarily frequent, since a Survey of any area in Latin America which omits such reference would be similar to Shakespeare's *Hamlet* with the omission of all reference to the Prince of Denmark. Criticism has been necessary, but it has seemed best to allow duly qualified nationals of the different areas to express themselves on debatable points, rather than advance the ideas of the author, who is a guest in the house of friends.

This Survey, so far as the author is aware,* is the first to be attempted for any area in Latin America. Its shortcomings may, therefore, enable other writers to avoid any errors which it may contain, and make their work more valuable. Should this be so, the writer will consider that he has been amply repaid for many hours of labour.

W. E. BROWNING.

Buenos Aires,
    Argentina.
      April 14th, 1928.

---

*The first Survey has recently been published entitled : *The Lowland Indians of Amazonia*, by K. G. Grubb, World Dominion Press, 1927 Price 5s.

CONTENTS

THE
RIVER PLATE REPUBLICS

I.

General Characteristics of the Region

1. *General Geographical Data.*

The three Republics which border the waters of the Rio de la Plata and its tributaries constitute a group of nations which are closely related owing to their geographical position, their close historical connection, and to the fact that in years to come they are destined to a common development. In a very special sense, as can be stated of no other group of Latin American nations, they are inter-related and dependent upon one another. Each one bears a very special relation to the great river system, whose muddy waters reach the Atlantic in a volume unsurpassed by that of any other river in the world save the Congo and the Amazon. Its waters are seven times greater in volume than those of the St. Lawrence.

This river, the Rio de la Plata, the " River of Silver," literally but generally incorrectly rendered in English as the " River Plate," is formed by the union of the waters of the Paraná, which in turn is formed by the Upper Paraná and the Paraguay, each with a number of important tributaries in the far interior, and the Uruguay. These two are the largest rivers in the world whose general flow is away from the Equator. It is, strictly speaking, an estuary of the Atlantic, but figures in all maps as a river.

The territory which it drains is equal to one-fourth of the area of the United States of America, and the system possesses about ten thousand miles of navigable waters. It provides a highway by which the otherwise almost inaccessible and but slightly explored regions of the heart of the continent may be penetrated, and it binds together the tropics and the temperate zone, establishing an outlet for the products of the far interior, which, on reaching tidal waters, are carried by the great transatlantic steamships to the most distant quarters of the globe. The name of this river is said to have been given it by Sebastian Cabot and his followers, who were sent out by the Spanish Crown in 1526 to build forts on the Uruguay, and to explore the interior. Silver ornaments bought from the Indians suggested the name, and it has since been known as the Rio de la Plata.

On the Iguazú, which is a tributary of the Upper Paraná, we find the second most important waterfalls of the world. They are exceeded in height and volume of water only by the Victoria Falls in Africa. The principal fall is fifty feet higher than the Falls of Niagara. Because of the location of these falls in the dense tropical jungle, far removed from the evidences of civilization, and because of their inherent beauty, they present one of the most picturesque and wonderful sights of the world. They are about 1,200 miles from Buenos Aires, and may be reached for the first part of the way by train; then by boat on the Upper Paraná to the mouth of the Iguazú; and finally through the jungle by motor or on horseback.

2. *General Historical Data.*

Probably the first European to reach this part of the world was Diego Garcia, a Portuguese pilot, who stayed for a few days in the mouth of the river in 1512. Three years later, Juan Diaz de Solis, a Spanish explorer, was commissioned by his sovereign to find a water route to the Pacific. He entered the estuary and later ascended the Uruguay, where he was murdered by the *Charrúa* Indians. In his honour the estuary was known for some years as the Rio de Solis, *i.e.*, Solis's River.

In 1520, the great Portuguese explorer Magellan anchored his little fleet in the estuary, while on his voyage of discovery round the world, and later, proceeding southwards, found and sailed through the Straits which bear his name. Sebastian Cabot was sent out in 1526 and established a number of forts along the river. Ten years later a great colonizing expedition arrived under the command of Pedro de Mendoza, and the first city of Buenos Aires (City of Fair Breezes) was founded. This was soon destroyed by the *Querandí* Indians and, in 1537, Asunción, now the capital of Paraguay, was founded, and for many years remained the centre of Spanish rule and influence in this region. Manuscripts may still be seen in the archives of the Paraguayan Government which date back to the year of the founding of this city, and others which refer to its subsequent history. When the full history of this region is written, these archives will prove to be of great value to the historian.

It was not until 1580 that Juan de Garay, coming down from Asunción with his followers, refounded Buenos Aires. From that time, owing to its greater accessibility, the latter gradually rose in importance until it became the centre of commercial and diplomatic relations with the mother country, Spain. From then onwards the importance of Asunción declined.

The history of the next two hundred years is a wearisome record of the rise and fall of successive aspirants to power, during which the population slowly increased. The struggle for freedom from the domination of the Old World began to show itself in the stirrings of a revolutionary spirit.

Others began to realize the importance of this region, and among these the Portuguese tried in vain to wrest it from Spain. In 1806, English forces under Sir John Beresford succeeded in getting into Buenos Aires, but after forty-five days they were driven out. An interesting fact in connection with the settlement made by Beresford was the interest shown by the patriot forces in taking over the printing press which the British army had set up in Montevideo. At that time, between the Rio Grande on the north of Mexico and Cape Horn, there were but nineteen presses, and all of them small, and the leaders of the separatist movements were eager to possess methods of greater and more effective communication among themselves and with the outer world. The press was brought to Buenos Aires, and, although its use was delayed until proper Spanish type could be secured, it did good service for many years.

A second English expedition took Montevideo during the following year, and attacked Buenos Aires. But the invaders were quickly and effectually repulsed by the Argentine patriots, and the entire region was then definitely evacuated by the British. Since that time the two countries have lived in complete harmony and mutual helpfulness.

3.   *The Argentina Federation Formed.*

On May 25th, 1810, a Declaration of Independence was proclaimed in Buenos Aires, and the first governing Council was formed, with Cornelio Saavedra as President. The first National Congress of Argentina was organized in 1825–26, and Bernardino Rivadavia was elected as the first President of the Federation.

During the first quarter of the nineteenth century there are records of many combats on land and sea. The great Argentine, José de San Martin, rose to power and, after liberating his own country from the power of Spain, crossed the Andes with his victorious troop and freed Chile and Perú. The same period also witnessed the gradual welding of many small and warring factions into the strong nationality to-day known as the Argentine Republic, and the separation of the modern Republics of Paraguay and Uruguay from the original vice-royalty and their organization as independent entities.

4. *The Rise of Paraguay.*

In a sense Paraguay may be said to be a nation without a history. Its past has rather been a tragedy in five acts, and those who have played the principal parts have been but few in number.

The first act included the stormy period of the conquest, in which the Spanish soldiers fought with the hardy Indian tribes, and, at length dispossessing them of their heritage of centuries, planted in the very heart of the continent the flaming colours of the Catholic Kings of Spain.

In the second act the colony thus formed freed itself from Spain, in 1811, and proclaimed its right to a free and independent existence. The principal actor of this period and of the immediately succeeding years was that most famous figure in the history of Paraguay, José Gaspar Rodriquez de Francia, generally known as Dr. Francia. As absolute Dictator, he ruled the country from 1816 till the time of his death in 1840. His ambition was to close Paraguay to all outside communication, and this he practically succeeded in doing.*

The third act is co-terminous with the rule of another Dictator who succeeded Francia, Cárlos Antonio López, who governed the country less despotically than his predecessor from 1841 to 1863. During his rule friendly relations were established with the neighbouring states and with the great foreign powers, and Paraguay seemed on its way to a high place among the nations.

---

* This ambition seems so incredible in these days when inter-communication is the great desire of the nations that one wishes it were possible to explain this determination. No doubt his psychological outlook was largely dominated by his lack of exact knowledge of the outer world. Then, too, he recognized that his little country was surrounded by much more powerful neighbours, and he, no doubt, feared that free communication with these adjacent countries might engender in their rulers a desire for the conquest of Paraguayan territory, and thus he abstained from forming what might have been eventually helpful relations through an exaggerated and mistaken patriotism. He will always remain a man of mystery, whose ideals perished with him. His methods may have been those best suited to his own day and the state of society by which he was surrounded, but of the correctness of these suppositions no one may now judge.

He was followed by his son, Francisco Solano López, generally known as the " Marshal," during whose pretentious and autocratic rule the country was plunged into one of the bloodiest wars that history records. At the beginning of the conflict, during which he fought the combined armies of Brazil, Argentina and Uruguay, the total population of Paraguay was estimated at 1,200,000. When the curtain went down on this fourth act through the throttling of his forces by the allied armies, and the death of López, bayoneted by a common soldier on the field of battle, there remained but two hundred and twenty thousand inhabitants. Of this number only twenty thousand were males, and the majority of these were boys, or men decrepit with age or disabled by wounds. This tremendous disparity in the numbers of each sex, eleven women to one male, brought in its train many unfortunate tendencies which have not yet, almost sixty years later, been completely eliminated. Illegitimacy is still tremendously high. Local authorities give it as 64.81 per cent. in Asunción, and we may assume that it is much higher in the country districts, although illegitimacy does not necessarily spell promiscuity. Among the humbler classes the woman is still the burden-bearer, and very largely the provider for the home.

The fifth act may be called the Period of Reconstruction : it began with the termination of the war in 1870, and continues until the present time. Gradually Paraguay is winning its way back to a place among modern nations and, with its immense natural resources and the enthusiasm of its present rulers, its future seems to be assured.

5. *The Rise of Uruguay.*

The comparatively small stretch of territory to the east of the River Uruguay, formerly known as *La Banda Oriental del Uruguay, i.e.,* the strip of land to the east of the River Uruguay, is the smallest of all the South American countries. During the colonial period it was a part of the vice-royalty of Buenos Aires, but was often invaded by Portuguese forces from Brazil in their repeated attempts to annex it to that country, and was once even definitely ceded to Portugal by Spain in a formal agreement made by the two Governments.

Because of this forced changing of loyalty to succeeding Governments, a sort of national consciousness was developed, and its peoples, though of the same Spanish stock as those who lived across the river in Argentina, began to assert their independence. Spain and Portugal finally formed an alliance in their attempt to uphold monarchical power in the region, and the Portuguese troops invaded Uruguay. They were driven out in 1814, under the leadership of the great José de Artigas, a daring plainsman who had risen to great popularity as a military leader, but who was subsequently expelled from the country and found refuge in Paraguay. From that date the country considered itself a separate nation. Invasions from both Argentina and Brazil continued, however, but in 1828 the independence of the little country was recognized by both these nations. Brazil had by this time revolted and secured its freedom from Portugal, and, hence, had lost all interest in coercing its small neighbours to continue under the yoke of monarchy from which its own independence had been so hardly won.

For many years, even until very recent times, bloody revolutions frequently retarded the progress of the country, the two principal opposing bands being known as the " Reds " and the " Whites "—a reminder to English readers of the Wars of the Roses. The " Whites " were in general the Church party, and the " Reds," who were radically opposed to the Church, were their opponents. These two historic political parties still dispute for supremacy in the elections, but, although the " Reds " have now been in power for many years, the bitterness of the past has largely disappeared. The new Constitution assures to each group its proportionate share in the control of the country and the offices at the disposal of the Government.

6. *Common Characteristics of the People.*

The area of the three Republics, 1,386,919 square miles, extends from well within the torrid zone to the cold ramparts of Cape Horn, about 55° south latitude. Within this vast area the most varied products of the earth may be produced. There are vast and valuable forests ; pastures capable of sustaining immense herds of sheep and cattle ; broad prairies that produce those great harvests of grain which go to feed the nations of the world ; gentle mountain slopes and hills which, at the touch of the hand of the skilled horticulturist, produce fruits of great variety ; while the mountains to the far west have mineral resources which have been scarcely touched.

The people of these three countries, save those of African descent who are exotic and not considered in this study, present common racial characteristics to a degree rarely equalled in other sections of the world. The autochthonous races proved inimical to the civilizing influences of the white man, and either withdrew into the far hinterland or were destroyed in their conflicts with the invader. Uruguay now has no Indians, although it was formerly the home of a number of fierce tribes, such as the *Charrúa* and the *Chaná*. In Argentina they are to be found only in the far south in Tierra del Fuego, where there are some three hundred of the *Ona* or *Yaghan* tribes, or in the *Chaco* to the far north, and in Paraguay only in the great forests and plains of the interior. As a result, there has been, especially in recent years, but little mixing of the white and Indian races, save in Paraguay, and even there it is the boast of the few remaining families who have descended from the early conquerors that they have kept their Spanish blood untainted. These families, however, are increasingly few in number, and the strong influence of the Indian strain is shown in the fact that the Guarani language is still the medium of conversation in the house and in ordinary speech, and has even been used in the National Congress.

The prevailing current of immigration has been from the Iberian Peninsula, and especially from Italy, and it may be said that, as in the United States of America, a new type of the Anglo-Saxon race, formed by the fusion of many elements, Latin as well as Nordic, found a fertile field for its development, so, in this particular region of South America, the Latin peoples of Southern Europe, mingling mostly in early years with women of Indian blood, and in later years, in many cases, with European people of other than Latin descent, have found a new home suited to their future development under climatic and social conditions congenial to their peculiar temperament.

Because of this common racial heritage, the moral and spiritual conditions which prevail in the three Republics of this region are very similar. There is the same type of Christianity, transplanted from Southern Europe at a period when the Church was not at a high spiritual level ; and religion to-day, as we shall see later on in this study, is no longer a matter of vital interest to more than a small minority of the people.

So much for the consideration of the area as a whole, and of some of the outstanding common characteristics of the people of the three countries. We must now consider briefly each Republic separately.

7. *The Modern Republic of Argentina.*

Argentina is a Federal Republic with a Constitution, adopted in 1853, which was very closely modelled upon that of the United States of America. It is composed of fourteen provinces, ten territories, and a federal district. Its total area is 1,153,119 square miles, a little over a third of that of the United States. For European readers this statement will be clearer if it is realized that this is equal to the combined areas of France, Germany, Italy, the United Kingdom, Ireland, Belgium, the Netherlands, Austria, Spain, Portugal, Switzerland,

Denmark, Poland and Lithuania, and leaves room for the smaller entities of Andorra, San Marino, Monaco, the Channel Islands, the Fiji Islands, the Bermudas, the Isle of Man, Liechtenstein, Gibraltar, and the District of Columbia, leaving still a considerable area to form a substantial country estate.

The population for 1927 was given as 10,348,189, of which number 2,280,000 were foreigners. One-fifth of the total population resides in Buenos Aires, the capital. Statisticians calculate that the population will be doubled within the next twenty-five years, owing to the low mortality and the high birth rate, the latter being considerably in excess of the former. Immigration is also a contributory factor in the rapid increase of the population, although the number of immigrants has recently declined, and in 1926 was only a hundred thousand.

The legislative power is vested in a Congress of two houses, a Senate and a Chamber of Deputies, the former with thirty members and the latter with a hundred and twenty. The Senators are elected by the legislatures of various provinces for a term of nine years, and the Deputies by a direct vote of the people. Each of these Deputies represents thirty thousand of the population. The President and Vice-President are elected for a term of six years. They must profess the Roman Catholic faith. The President must have an income of at least £400, and receives a salary of a little over £6,000 a year. Roman Catholicism is the official religion of the State, but there is complete tolerance of all other forms of worship. The Governors of the provinces are elected by the people, and the President appoints those of the territories, and also the Mayor or Governor of the federal district. Military service is compulsory, and there is a standing army of twenty thousand, with a possible mobilization of a hundred and twenty thousand, a navy of forty vessels, and a naval reserve of 3,500 men. Argentina has a well organized and extensive air service, and its aeroplanes are in constant use by the army in its work of inspection throughout the Republic. A regular postal service is maintained with Montevideo. Aeroplanes now overtake transatlantic liners at the most eastern point of Brazil, thus shortening the trip for mails to Europe by four or five days. Plans are now being considered for the establishment of a regular air-mail service to Spain and France. Each province legislates for its own internal affairs, but all unite in forming the Federal Government which enacts and carries into effect legislation of common interest.

For many years of its early history the principal port and province, Buenos Aires, carried on a struggle with the rest of the country, and even to-day there is a difference in the psychology of the Argentine citizen between the *Porteños*, or port-dwellers, and the dwellers in the camp or open country. The business, political, literary and intellectual life of the country centres to an unusual degree, even for a Latin country, in the capital, and gives it an importance comparable to that of Paris or Rome. Buenos Aires is the gateway through which most imports and exports pass, including those of Paraguay. It maintains its supremacy by continually drawing people from the interior. Other important export towns are Rosario, Santa Fé, and Bahia Blanca. The great landed proprietors naturally live in the capital and spend in it the income from their estates. These are left to the care of subordinates, who take all they can secure from those below them. Buenos Aires is now the second Latin capital of the world, surpassed only by Paris, and destined possibly to take the first place among Latin cities.*

The Province of Buenos Aires, generally known as the " Queen Province," has an area of 117,777 square miles, almost equal to that of Great Britain and Ireland, and a population of about three million. The capital is La Plata, near the mouth of the river, about an hour's journey from Buenos Aires by express train. This city has an unusually fine Museum of Natural History and one of the

---

* This city is in almost the same latitude as Cape Town, and so a large part of Argentina lies further south than the southernmost point of Africa.

five universities of the country, provided with a well-equipped astronomical observatory. The Province, as will be seen by reference to the map, is crossed by many railways, so that every district is in close touch with the federal capital. In all Argentina there are about forty thousand kilometres of railway (25,000 miles) or forty-three per cent. of the total mileage in South America. Most of these railways are British owned, and there are also many British banks and well established commercial houses in Buenos Aires. British influence is very strong and beneficial throughout the Republic. The total British investments in Argentina are estimated at £500,000,000 and are greater than those of any other investing country. The total annual foreign trade of the Republic amounts to 1,590,000,000 gold dollars, or over fifty per cent. of that of all South America.

Certain select society groups, because of intensive development, are very largely dominated by worldly interests and a material interpretation of life. Patriotism for the average Argentine amounts almost to a mania, and there is a real passion for the further development of the resources of the country and the adornment of its capital. Life here has all the glitter of European capitals. The visitor finds splendid boulevards, some of the finest theatres in the world, open-air cafés on the sidewalks, up-to-date toilettes, and hears the whirl of the most expensive motor-cars, notes the arrival of transatlantic and transcontinental mails by aeroplane and ocean liner, and feels that he is enjoying full twentieth century experiences, or even a foretaste of the twenty-first.

The recent general elections, held on Sunday, April 1st, 1928, have demonstrated that there exists a high degree of civic culture among the people of Argentina, since they were carried through without any special disturbance of the public peace. In the federal capital, out of 303,712 entitled to exercise the right of suffrage, 277,401 voted, or 91.33 per cent. This is probably a record for Argentina, and is a high average in any country.

The two leading political parties, so far as a foreigner can discover, are merely divisions of the strong Liberal or Radical Party. These two parties are generally designated as the "Personalist" and the "Anti-Personalist," the former with decided leanings towards the proletariat, the other somewhat less democratic.

Next in importance among the political parties is the "Socialist" group, which stands for complete separation of Church and State, increased educational facilities for the children of the poor, a divorce law as the necessary complement of the existing civil marriage law, and other general legislation which favours the working man. This party is strong and is increasingly influential, exercising a wholesome influence upon the other parties by keeping its important tenets always before the voters.

In addition to the above, there is a "Public Health" Party and a "Communist" Party, the latter of which is divided into three separate groups, each with its own candidates and programme.

8. *The Modern Republic of Uruguay.*

Uruguay is the smallest of all the South American republics, with an area of 72,153 square miles, nearly one and a half times the size of England, and is wedged in between its two mighty neighbours, Argentina and Brazil. It has been compared to a garden plot between two great estates. The population is over one million seven hundred thousand, one-quarter of whom reside in the capital, Montevideo.

The climatic conditions are similar to those which prevail across the river in Argentina, though Montevideo is cooler in summer. Because of its extensive beaches of clean white sand, the hospitality of its people and the attraction of its modern hotels, the capital and its suburbs have become one of the most popular sea-side resorts in South America.

Uruguay is a centralized Republic and elects its President through the General Assembly. The country is divided into departments, and these are sub-divided into sections and districts. By the terms of the new Constitution, which was promulgated in January, 1918, there is a complete separation of Church and State and all religions are declared equal before the law. There are two houses in the Congress, the Senate and the Deputies, and the executive power is divided between the President of the Republic and a National Council of Administration. The Departments or Ministries of Foreign Relations, War, Navy and Interior, are under the direct control of the President. The other Departments of the Government are controlled by the Council, which is composed of nine members.

The principal industry in Uruguay is stock-raising and the shipment of its products, though agriculture is gradually increasing. Montevideo is recognized as one of the most important cultural centres of Latin America, and, because of its advanced and often daring legislation, the country is regarded as the social laboratory of South American republics. Its intellectual leaders take a prominent part in all continental and world social and civic movements, and its capital, often called the Geneva or the Hague of the Americas, is the recognized centre for the celebration of international Congresses of all kinds, especially those which deal with matters purely American.

The health of the country may be judged from the fact that in 1926 the death rate was 10.36 per thousand, one of the lowest rates in the world.

The British colony in Uruguay has always been strong and influential and British investments reach a high figure. Railways and banks represent a large proportion of this invested capital. There is an unusually good British school in Montevideo, the corner stone of which was laid by H.R.H. the Prince of Wales in 1925. There is also a British hospital and other evidences of British wealth and influence.

9. *The Modern Republic of Paraguay.*

Paraguay, which is often referred to as the " Mesopotamia of South America," lies well up in the interior, almost surrounded by the great rivers which pour their flood into the Rio de la Plata. It has an area of 161,647 square miles, about treble that of England, though its boundaries with Bolivia are still in dispute and, in consequence, no exact and definite statement can be made of its size. The population is estimated at a little less than a million : that is to say, it has again acquired the population it had at the beginning of the war of 1865 already mentioned. The capital, Asunción, has less than a hundred thousand inhabitants, or about ten per cent. of the entire population. The Constitution is almost exactly the same as that of the Argentine Republic, except that Paraguay is a centralized Republic like Uruguay, altogether ruled from its capital. Indians, both civilized and savage, and those who have Indian blood in their veins, form the bulk of the population. The uncivilized tribes now form but a small minority of the whole. One of the principal industries is the production and export of Paraguayan tea, generally known as *mate*. The annual production of this herb exceeds 2,500,000 pounds, and provides employment for thousands of men and women.

Rice, sugar, tobacco and cotton are also being increasingly cultivated, and the results, both as to quantity and quality, prove that the soil and the climate of Paraguay are admirably suited for their production. Quebracho extract for tanning, and various kinds of timber for building purposes, are exported in great quantities.

It is, however, in the production of fruit that Paraguay could rival any country in the world. The soil and climate, combined with human intelligence, could easily convert the entire country into a vast orchard, capable of supplying not only the home market but also Buenos Aires and Montevideo and, if packing facilities were provided, Europe and the United States as well.

The orange tree, which was first introduced by the Jesuit missionaries who entered the country early in the seventeenth century, seems to have found a soil and climate in Paraguay particularly suited to its growth, which much impresses the stranger to the country. The jungles, too, are golden with the fruit of the wild variety. With little or no cultivation the domestic species produces thousands of tons of delightful fruit which is eagerly sought after in the markets of the coast. The exportation during a single year amounts to over a hundred and fifty million oranges. Steamers loaded with only this golden fruit, piled high on the decks, race down the great rivers to unload in the docks of Buenos Aires and Montevideo.

Owing to the hitherto unsettled political situation, although very few regions offer such natural advantages for the prosecution of this industry, cattle-raising is but in its infancy. There is abundance of water and nutritious grazing may be found in all parts of the country. Already there are large herds of cattle destined for the coastal packing houses and for the markets of Europe and North America.

There can be little question as to the natural advantages and the future possibilities of the country, but, before Paraguay can become a strong and influential entity among nations, some of the conditions which have hindered progress in the past must be overcome.

One of the chief obstacles to the progress of Paraguay, which is also common to Argentina and other Latin American countries, is the system of *latifundia*. Enormous tracts of land have been secured and are held to-day, very often by foreigners. One may travel for an entire day along any one of the great water routes and be told that all the land on one bank of the river, if not on both, belongs to one man or to one family, and that from the river it stretches for many leagues into the interior, embracing forests and pasture lands of an almost incalculable value. It is not uncommon to hear of tracts that cover hundreds of square miles of territory. Many owners indeed do not know the exact amount of their holdings.

The use of a depreciated currency also restricts foreign investments and hinders progress.   At the present time, the Paraguayan peso, which is the unit of value, is worth only about one penny in British currency, or forty-five pesos to the American dollar, and the tendency in the last few years has been downward.   At such a rate prices are ridiculously high in terms of local currency, and for a comparatively small sum in American gold or pounds sterling one may enter the ranks of Paraguayan millionaires.

It is mainly due to the lack of funds that asylums, hospitals and other benevolent institutions leave much to be desired in their equipment and administration.

10.   *The Racial Situation.*

There is a possibility that, owing to the restriction on immigration from Italy and to the increase of immigration from Northern Europe following the Great War, the racial preponderance in this area, and especially in Argentina, may in the future be gradually changed.   There is already a numerous Teutonic population in each of these Republics, and the number of incoming prospective citizens from Germany and Poland is each year becoming greater.   In Argentina in 1927 out of a total of 161,940 immigrants, belonging to ninety-five nationalities, 69,000 were Italians, 34,000 were Spaniards and 18,000 were Poles.

In 1925, the total number of immigrants was only 34,585, of whom 16,641 were Italians, 8,056 Spaniards, 4,252 Poles, 1,309 Germans, and only five British, the remaining 4,322 coming from other scattered nationalities.   The German and Polish immigration into Paraguay has been particularly heavy in recent years, but no exact statistics can be given.   There is a difference in the character of the immigrants since the War, due to the fact that the newcomers are likely to settle down in the country and form racial groups. For instance, the Germans, Poles and others in search of new and permanent homes will do much towards the development of the vast farming and grazing areas now unoccupied. In all three countries lodging is provided for a few days to all new arrivals, in the Immigrants' Hotels, and these serve as distributing centres whence these new citizens are sent on to their final destinations. While these lines are being written the daily press of Buenos Aires calls attention to the fact that the Immigrants' Hotel in this city is overflowing with 2,800 people. Many who have exceeded the five days allowed them, having no place to go to and being unable to find employment, are generously permitted to over-stay their time and are cared for at public expense. Some remain for a month, or more, before finding work or friends. Most of these 2,800 immigrants are young men; women immigrants number two hundred only. As in previous years, the majority are Italians, followed by Spaniards, Poles, Germans, Russians, Jugoslavs, Czechoslovaks, etc. The Italians and Spaniards soon find work, due to their knowledge of the language. The Germans are generally cared for by their own large colony, and Jews are looked after by the Jewish Colonization Society. The other races mentioned find difficulty in securing work, owing to the fact that they do not know the language and generally have no relatives or friends to receive them.

An examination of recent statistics shows that the tendency among immigrants is largely toward finding work and settling down in agricultural districts where vast areas are given over to the growth of cereals, to the cultivation of grapes used for making wine, to the raising of cattle on the prairies as in Paraguay, and to the production of sugar in the warmer districts, as in the Province of Tucumán in Argentina.

It is interesting to note that in Argentina the total number of immigrants from 1857 to 1924 was 5,481,276, of which 64,426 were British and only 9,028 were from the United States of America. Italy sent 2,604,029, Spain 1,780,295, France 226,894, Germany 100,688. The remainder belonged to many other nationalities.

It has been estimated that if all her arable land were properly cultivated Argentina alone could support a population of a hundred million and, at the same time, export foodstuffs for an equal number outside.

One undesirable result of this influx of immigrants has been the growth of socialism and communism. Strikes, led by communists, have been frequent. The socialist party is particularly strong in Argentina and advocates some very sane and important principles, such as the complete separation of Church and State, increased educational facilities for the proletariat, better housing for workmen, and stricter legislation in regard to hours of work. Labour is thoroughly organized and has its international affiliations. For example, a strike ordered by one of the smaller organizations, perhaps caused by the dismissal of an incompetent or insubordinate workman, may spread to other sympathizing organizations, with the result that the industries of a city or of the whole country become quickly paralysed. This spirit has spread even to the student class, and it is not an unusual event for the university doors to be closed and barred against the entrance of its own authorities. The student strikes at times have spread throughout the countries under review, and, until the demands of the students have been met, have resulted in the closing of all universities and secondary schools.

11. *Education and General Culture.*

In matters of education there is no doubt that Argentina, closely followed by Uruguay, leads Latin America. Paraguay is considerably behind the other two countries in this respect. The educational systems of these Republics are well organized. The capitals and larger cities possess excellent schools of all grades, taught by teachers who are well prepared in the technique of instruction. In the country districts, as in all new countries, there remains much to be done to bring the equipment and instruction up to the grade of that in the larger centres. There are five universities in Argentina, and one each in Paraguay and Uruguay. The University of Córdoba is one of the oldest in the Western Hemisphere, having been founded in 1572, or forty-four years before the founding of Harvard, the oldest university in the United States of America.

In Paraguay and Uruguay the entire educational system is under the control of the central Government and includes all grades of work, from kindergarten to university courses. In Argentina, the provincial Governments are responsible for primary education, and the Federal Government for secondary. The schools in the federal district and in the ten territories are under the jurisdiction of the National Council of Education which, although a dependency of the Ministry of Public Instruction, is practically autonomous. This Council is guided by a law, also the model for provincial legislation, which establishes compulsory free education, graded suitably for children of six to fourteen years of age.

As a matter of fact, although primary education is made compulsory, should all children of school age present themselves for registration, there would be insufficient schools for their accommodation. In Buenos Aires there are many who, for this reason, do not attend school, and the same is true also of Montevideo and Asunción ; yet in each of these three countries the capital is especially favoured in the matter of school accommodation. Statistics as to illiteracy are scant and often misleading, but it is evidently true that Argentina stands first among all the countries of Latin America as regards the low percentage of analphabets, closely followed by Uruguay, with Paraguay considerably behind these two.

As in all Latin countries, the educational system is subordinate to the requirements of the university degree, and primary and secondary education are primarily designed with a view to passing the entrance examination to the University Faculty. The university is merely a dispenser of the degrees required for entering upon a professional career, and is of little cultural

value.*   There are also, particularly in Argentina, a
large number of schools for special instruction, such
as normal schools, primary schools for adults, schools
for backward children, holiday schools, schools of
modern languages, institutes of physical training,
institutes for the deaf and dumb, blind, etc., a national
academy of fine arts, a national school of arts, a national
conservatory of music and recitation, and a large
number of private institutions for various other objects.
Among these last are schools of the foreign communities,
such as British, American, German, French and
Italian schools.

The universities of Argentina are autonomous,
with certain limitations, each with its governing body
constituted by a council of delegates from each faculty.
The Rector or President is elected by the assembly
of professors for a term of three or more years.   Each
faculty is ruled by its academic council, and by the
dean elected by the professional staff, and, in some
cases, by a student electorate, which has the right to
send representatives to take part in the sessions and
express opinions on the subjects discussed.

This system has produced a large number of
distinguished scholars and writers, although, if
compared with the total population of the country,
altogether too few.   Though the standard of instruction
is high, the schools do not tend to build up character.
The head of one of these universities is quoted as
saying : " We are able to instruct, but we do not
seem to be able to form men.   We cannot educate."
Another writes : " We turn out good scholars but,
for some reason, we do not produce good citizens."
A President of the Republic of Paraguay recently
wrote :

" Our secondary education is lacking on the moral
side.   Our young men learn many things, but we do
not inculcate in them the essential principles of human

---

* Jewesses are rapidly increasing in number on the staffs of the
public schools, in some cases amounting to a monopoly.   They are
well trained in the normal schools and, since religious instruction is
debarred from schools, there is no sectarian test.

conduct. Furthermore, the encyclopedic learning which fills their brains inspires a disdain of all activities which are not puerile or an empty lyricism.

" Beardless youths get possession of daily papers and magazines and write on social, literary, and historical themes, with all the gravity of academicians grown grey over their books.

" This is not the fault of the youths, whose ambitions are noble, but somewhat mistaken, simply because their teachers have not been able to inculcate in them that sense of reality which is essential.

" Unfortunately, those who have the care of souls are more interested in their work of proselytizing than in elevating the mind of our youth to a noble and austere conception of the reality of life."*

The prevailing foreign influence in the intellectual life of these Republics, as in all Latin America, is French, and French literature is the most widely read. Many of the leaders of thought publicly apostrophize France as their spiritual and intellectual mother, and Paris is the Mecca to which all strive to make at least one pilgrimage. English literature is appreciated by but a few, and has had but little influence in moulding forms of thought. German is even less sought after, although works in that language are read by many professionals, such as physicians, engineers, etc.

12.   *Sanitation and Public Health.*

In the capital cities sanitation is advanced, and follows the lines of the most recent legislation. This is especially true in Buenos Aires and Montevideo. In the smaller towns and country districts much has yet to be done to bring them into line with the large centres. Yellow fever, formerly a scourge throughout South America, has been exterminated. Lepers are to be found in the three countries, and the disease is believed to be spreading. There are some two hundred

---

* Eusebio Ayala. Quoted in *La Mañana*, Montevideo, April 16th, 1922.

lepers in Uruguay, while in both Argentina and Paraguay the number is much greater. Segregation is not obligatory, but asylums or hospitals are provided for those who desire to receive free care and treatment About twenty are thus cared for in Montevideo, some two hundred in Buenos Aires and about fifty in Asunción. Chaulmoogra oil has been used, but with little success. There is no widespread horror of the disease, and the medical faculty does not seem to be concerned at its presence and probable increase. Lepers are to be found among beggars and street vendors. They travel in public conveyances, and many are interned by their families in their own homes.

Venereal diseases are frightfully prevalent, and one may read great placards in the public streets urging the necessity of taking prophylactic and therapeutic measures.

In the capital cities there are many physicians who would be an honour to the profession in any country. In Argentina and Uruguay there is a well-organized system of hospitals, first-aid service, etc., but the smaller towns and country districts, since physicians will not leave the larger cities for the country or small town practice, are woefully lacking in these advantages. As a result, in the country districts there are many quack physicians, and men and women who do a flourishing business in collecting and distilling certain herbs with curative properties. The country districts are often lacking too in chemist shops, with the result that the unfortunate people are left to the tender mercies of the quack and vendor of patent medicines. There are but few foreign physicians, even in the great cities, for the reason that the laws for the revalidation of diplomas or the passing of examinations are so strict that they effectually exclude all those who have not been trained in the local schools of medicine. The graduates of the best British and American medical schools, even after years of successful practice, must submit to an examination in Spanish in the local medical school on the entire course of medical study. It is frankly admitted that everything legally possible will be done to prevent the passing of the test and the securing of permission to practise. This is also true in other faculties, as law, dentistry, and pharmacy.

In Paraguay, hookworm has been widely prevalent, but, as a result of the energetic and successful activities of representatives of the Rockefeller Foundation, the disease should shortly be eradicated. Paludic fevers are also prevalent in Paraguay and the north of Argentina, but, as a result of prophylactic measures, they tend to disappear. There are occasional cases of bubonic plague, generally among recently arrived immigrants or sailors, and any spread of the disease is quickly prevented by strict segregation in the hospitals for contagious diseases.

The leading foreign communities generally establish their own hospitals. The British hospitals at Buenos Aires and Montevideo are among the best in these cities, with full staffs of competent physicians and well-trained nurses. In Buenos Aires the medical staff of the hospital is principally British, both the physicians in charge and the head nurse being of that nationality. In Montevideo, there is no British physician on the staff, but the head nurse is British and the majority of the other nurses are Anglo-Argentines, trained in the hospital itself. The head physician and all his assistants are Uruguayans.

This region is lacking in training schools for nurses. This is due to the fact that the work is looked on as menial, rather than professional, and therefore few young women of the upper social classes present themselves as candidates. The nursing in the State hospitals of Argentina and Paraguay is, for the most part, in the hands of Sisters of Mercy.

11.

The Religious Life

1. *Legislation as to Religion.*

In Argentina and Paraguay the Roman Catholic Church is the official Church, but there is complete liberty of worship and the persecution of dissidents is now unknown. The Church is a social rather than a spiritual power. The apparent policy of the politicians is to let it alone so long as it does not interfere with matters of State. Some of them, because of its antiquity or because of family associations, even accord it a sort of respect. For the most part this Church is not a spiritual power, nor are its ministers such as to induce a soul in tribulation willingly to go to them for help and consolation.

In Uruguay, after years of struggle, a complete separation of Church and State was brought about, and Article III. of the Constitution, which was adopted in 1918, reads as follows :—

" All forms of religious worship are free in Uruguay. The State sustains no religion whatever. It recognizes that the Roman Catholic Church has control over all church buildings which, in part or entirely, have been erected with funds contributed from the national treasury, excepting only the chapels destined to the services of hospitals, asylums, prisons or other public institutions. It declares, likewise, that all church buildings which have been consecrated to worship by the different religions are exempt from the payment of taxes."

In this Republic in early years the Roman Catholic Church was unusually intolerant and bigoted, and this alienated the loyalty of a very large part of the community. To-day, most of the men who occupy

C

positions of large political influence are professedly
atheists or, at best, agnostics, and every attempt is
made to exclude the name of God, and all reference to
Christianity, from State documents and even from the
daily papers. The Church, having sowed to the wind,
now reaps the whirlwind.

The separation which compelled the Church to
develop on its own resources of life and money has
both purified and consolidated the activities of the
Church party. However, owing to the liberal teaching
outside and the general influence of university life,
the Church will continue to lose in membership.

In Argentina, although the Roman Catholic Church
is recognized as the official Church, it has been largely
shorn of its power. The State reserves to itself the
right to nominate the Bishops and the Archbishop,
the nominations to be ratified by the Vatican. Only
recently the position of Archbishop remained vacant
for some years because the Government and the
Vatican could not agree on the candidate proposed
by the former.

The Constitution confines itself to the laconic
declaration that " the Federal Government sustains
the Roman Catholic Apostolic form of worship,"
and further declares that one of the requisites of
candidates to the Presidency or Vice-Presidency is
that they should belong to " the Roman Catholic
Apostolic Communion."

The Constitution of Paraguay Article IV. reads :

" The religion of the State is the Apostolic Roman
Catholic ; the head of the Church must be a Paraguayan ; however, the Congress shall not prohibit
the free exercise of any other religion in the territory
of the Republic."

Article VI., which refers to the guarantees and
rights of the citizens, declares, among other things,
that every one will be permitted to " publish his
ideas through the press, to use and dispose of his
property for useful purposes, to profess freely his
form of worship, to teach and learn."

The Government sustains certain departments of

the Church, but this support must be altogether inadequate, since the entire amount contributed by the Government for the support of the Church, in a recent year, was but 278,400 pesos (about £1,145), while for the upkeep of army and navy the amount voted was 14,930,854 pesos.

Because of this small income, if for no other reason, it is not surprising that the Roman Catholic Church has done so little toward the building up of a strong and useful organization in Paraguay. It is stated that there are only eighty-four priests in the country. Forty of this number live in the capital, and many of them occupy positions as chaplains, teachers, etc. This means that the remaining eight hundred thousand of the population scattered over the whole country, where means of communication are lacking or are of the poorest, are left to the care of but forty spiritual advisers. Even if each of these men had the learning and executive ability of Ignatius de Loyola, or the fiery zeal of Peter the Hermit, his task would still be greater than his powers.

2. *Marriage and Cemetery Laws*.

In all three Republics the only legal marriage is by civil contract, though the contracting parties may afterwards have their union blessed by the Church of their preference. For the legitimization of children and in the matter of inheritances, however, only the civil ceremony is taken into account, and, without it, save in special cases provided for in the law, all children are considered illegitimate and cannot inherit.

The cemeteries belong to the State and are open to all, irrespective of creed. Any national or religious group may, if it so desires, by conforming to certain stipulations of the law, maintain its own burial grounds. The British and the German communities generally have their own cemeteries, administered by a Board of Managers. Before 1914, these two communities sometimes united in this matter. The American community, which is generally small in number, is, as a rule, given the use of the British cemetery for the burial of its dead.

3. *The Social Situation.*

In these countries, as in all Latin America, personal moral delinquency is in no case an obstacle to public service. In considering an application for any position, high or low, in the public service, what a man is in private life matters not a whit. This doctrine, no doubt, has its roots in the teaching of the Church that the priest is to be reverenced, as such, no matter what his private life may be. He officiates as a priest, not as an individual. In like manner the public official is accepted as such, and that notwithstanding the fact that, judged from the Anglo-Saxon and Protestant code of ethics, his private life is far below the level of even common morality.

The Church has seldom interested itself in matters of social betterment. A few years ago, however, some of the clergy of Buenos Aires launched a campaign on behalf of better houses for the labouring man, and raised a fund of several millions of pesos. The Bishop who headed this movement, and became very popular in the country because of his social activities, was soon afterwards proposed by the Government for the position of Archbishop; but the appointment was never endorsed by the Vatican, and the Bishop was quietly transferred to other work. Evidently his interest in social betterment did not, in the estimation of his ecclesiastical superiors, fit him for the position of head of the Church in Argentina.

As a rule, the women, especially those of the upper social classes, are nominally supporters of the Church. That the men of Argentina and Paraguay are tolerant to the presence and work of the Church is due largely to their innate courtesy to their women folk. In Uruguay, there is but little courtesy shown by the leaders of the Liberal political party now in power, except such as is demanded by the letter of the law.

4. *The Religious Situation discussed by Nationals.*

The writer, perhaps more fully than many others who, like him, have spent long years in South America and know something of the work of the Roman Catholic Church in the past and its possibilities for the future, desires and always endeavours to give that Church full credit for what it has accomplished. It is for this reason that he prefers to quote from citizens of these countries when direct criticisms of the dominant Church are necessary. Moreover, from those criticisms so often found in the current literature of the various countries, he prefers to choose only those which have been voiced by responsible parties, and to ignore all statements made in the heat of political passion, at the time of hotly contested elections, or by those whose judgment, for personal reasons, may be warped or founded on a misapprehension. For these reasons, in order to throw light on the religious situation in the region under review, competent and well-known authorities, citizens of the country, are quoted, and the reader is left to judge for himself the value of their statements.

(*a*) An Argentine Lawyer.

The first to be quoted is an outstanding educator in the Argentine Republic, a lawyer and not a member of any Protestant Church. Questioned as to the influence of religion in Argentina, he writes :

1. " Religion as such does not influence, and I doubt that it ever has seriously interested, the lives of our people. So-called believers never could see in it other than rites and ceremonies ; unbelievers, nothing better than superstition. Consequently, religion has never furnished to the first-named any efficient control of conduct, nor to the second any matter worthy of serious attention. Hence it is that the expressions of religious fidelity, which now and again appear on the pages of our histories, either have no real significance, are children of a false historical

interpretation, or respond to the desire to favour the continuance of certain practices, which, in spite of everything to be said against them, are deemed useful for the weaker vessels of society, *i.e.*, for women and children.

2. " Why may it be that religion has so small an influence on the people of these countries ? Why have they never taken it seriously ? These are more than serious questions. To answer them adequately requires an amount of study which at present I cannot dedicate to them. I will however say that related thereto are the following factors :

(*a*) " Our Græco-Roman antecedents on religious matters, profoundly formalistic and widely separate from the God concept.

(*b*) " The psychology of the Spanish people which we have inherited, a psychology which was shaped or mis-shaped through eight centuries of a death struggle with Islam. That struggle which made the Cross the undoubted and incontrovertible symbol of national unity in Spain, throughout the Middle Ages, suppressed all religious speculation, petrifying and perverting Christianity, making of it more a matter of politics than of religion, more an emblem of war than of peace.

(*c*) " With the organization of the conquest of South America which, say of it what one will, and postulate the exceptions that one may, was fundamentally encouraged and sustained by material motives.

(*d*) " With our cosmopolitanism, which has confounded all races and religions, inevitably obliging us to an absolute toleration, which has developed in its finality to an equally absolute indifference.

(*e*) " With our condition of a people in embryo, which has driven universal preoccupation to the field of utilitarianism.

" Of a truth, the two ultimate factors might have been overcome, had any potent spiritual factors been riveted to our soil, as in the case of the United States of America. Since none such existed, these factors have only accentuated the evil.

" In view of these reasons, it is open to affirmation that, rather than Protestantism, it is Roman Catholicism which has reason to complain of the small favour with which it is viewed. Not long since, Monsignore Baudrillat, expounding his impressions gathered in Argentina, emphasized the religious coldness here. Recently a phrase has been attributed to Doctor Alvear (Argentine President) which I consider of absolute precision : ' I have become acquainted with Catholics in France, but I have never met a single Catholic in Argentina.' "

(b) An Argentine Educator.

The second national writer to be quoted here is also an educationalist, and one of the best known writers on educational subjects in Latin America. He is neither a Protestant nor a Roman Catholic, but his life and interested helpfulness in all good movements indicate that he is a Christian.

In the course of a public address recently delivered in Buenos Aires, he declared :

" The Catholic branch of Christianity in the Latin countries is one of the crudest forms of religious faiths. It appeals chiefly to narrow and selfish motives, and consequently attracts very few really superior characters.

" Its priesthood is far from enjoying the same social standing as ministers do in the Anglo-Saxon countries. Very few young men of high moral type freely choose that calling. The Roman Catholic theological seminaries are being more and more deserted, and the ecclesiastical authorities are at pains to fill their ranks. They fish their men from among orphans and poor widows' sons, at the price of a pittance, but the local seminaries cannot supply all the priests needed by the Church. Therefore a large part of them are foreigners—Spaniards and Italians—painfully ignorant and totally foreign to our feelings and ideals.

" Men of moral stamina generally drift away from

religious activities as soon as they discover that the
Roman Catholic Church is chiefly a power-seeking
institution, and that ignorance and superstition are
her most fruitful allies.

" Of course, the women—especially those belonging
to the smart set—are religion's chief supporters.
Most of them are sincere believers in the Church.
This explains the fact that almost any social work
conducted by women in these countries has a religious
character. When I say religious character, I refer
especially to the ecclesiastical connection between
such movements and Church and priest, rather than
to purely religious motives by which their organizers
may be prompted. Institutions governed by women
are looked upon by the priests as a proper ground for
proselytizing. Applicants for assistance at such
institutions have to avow the Roman Catholic faith
and closely observe its practices. Even at city hospitals
cases are known of Sisters denying help to inmates
who do not submit to ritualistic ceremonies.

" Speaking broadly, men are non-religious, and I
must declare that the great majority of men who
have distinguished themselves in public service are
men without Church connection. I will go so far as
to state here that a sort of suspicion lingers about a
Churchman, for people know that loyalty to the
Roman Catholic Church does not always mean loyalty
to what is right and just. . . . However, no matter
how out of sympathy a man may feel with the Roman
Catholic Church, the foundation principles of Christianity often find a sympathetic response from him.
That is not a general fact, however, for, in the minds
of educated men, there is often no place left where
sound religious ideas may develop. With them even
morality has lost its religious foundations. In such
cases morality derives its strength from a sense of
honour or from patriotic motives. You will find
hundreds of men ready to help carry their neighbours'
burdens, whose acts are prompted not by religious
motives but by an unmixed sense of duty and a pure
desire to do good. Of course, you will rightly say

that this is religion, and I admit it is. But I think you accomplish little in your work if you attempt to bring such men back to their lost faith. Proselytizing is a much discredited process because in doing it the Roman Catholic priest seeks chiefly power for his organization. As you know, there are no sects in Roman Catholicism. People brought under Roman Catholic dogmas have little conception of personal religious freedom, and they look at denominations as contending powers rather than as expressions of personal interpretations of religious faith. Therefore, any attempt at religious propaganda, however disinterested, will be construed as an attempt to weaken the power of the Church for the aggrandizement of another. The slightest suspicion that you are doing this will deprive you of some authority, even among the bitterest enemies of the Roman Catholic Church.

"Whoever comes to South America with the intention of furthering the interests of dogmatism, or of propagating theological controversy, will meet with failure. Those questions do not interest the South American youth and, in my opinion, they have ceased to interest the whole Latin race. And here is presented the great opportunity for those who have full faith in the regenerating power of the social message of the Gospel. If there is anything that has really interested these last two generations in South America, from the Christian point of view, it has been the works of Tolstoy. If there is anything to-day in the Anglo-Saxon countries which can interest the young men here, when they become acquainted with it, it is without doubt the point of view of men like Rauschen-busch. The young men of South America will always be disposed to listen with attention to him who speaks of these things. The question of ecclesiastical organization does not interest him ; whether it be the Episcopal régime, the Presbyterian, or the Congregational, it is a matter of indifference to him. He does not believe in the Church, feels no need for it, and is accustomed to ignore its existence. Still less can his interest be aroused in ancient disputes about predestination, free-will, eucharistic transubstantiation, auricular confession, or clerical celibacy. These are questions of the sixteenth century which have no message for the twentieth. But the regenerating power of the Gospel, yes. Jesus, Liberator of Man, will always find a place in our hearts."

(c) The President of an Argentine University.

On the other hand, it is a pleasure to quote a recent writer, the President of the University of Buenos Aires,* who has developed, in his most recent book to which he gives the title *The Christ Invisible*. his philosophy of religion and his personal position as a Christian. It is in a sense an epoch-making book in this region, and is sure to exercise a wide influence because of the standing of the writer among the best-known of the intelligentsia of the day.

The book is in the form of conversations with a Bishop of the Roman Catholic Church. Only a brief summary can be given here, to lead up to the final and splendid declaration of his own faith and attitude toward the adherents of other faiths. In one conversation he presents the problem of the harmony of the four Gospels written from four distinct viewpoints. Can they be harmonized? Are they essentially contradictory? There enters also the danger of individual interpretation of the Gospels and the necessity of relying on the Church's interpretation. They discuss the difficulties of the language of the Gospels, of possible errors in copying, of the superficial lack of harmony in the manner of expression of Jesus in the different Gospels. He cites opinions of other thinkers, he quotes the Biblical Cyclopedia, and the old clergyman reproaches him for bringing in Protestant evidence. He gives a theosophist's opinion, and is still more condemned because of the " bad lawyer " he brings in.

---

* A local review has proclaimed him as " one of the most prolific intellects of Latin America," and this, in view of his tremendous literary output during the past quarter of a century, is probably correct.

Since the Bishop is not convinced, he proposes another solution. "One single symbol," he says, "the parable of the Master." He goes on to explain that the Master's life was a parable in action, His miracles, His words, His prayers. He who would hear Jesus' words as He spoke them in Galilee must study his own life, make his own life a parable of Jesus. He puts into the miracles of Jesus a spiritual significance which is rather unusual. To him Jesus was not only a physician of the body, but a physician of the soul. The desire to forgive and to create a new heart was always greater than the desire to heal a broken body. To-day the transformation of withered minds and hearts is of greater significance than the transforming of withered limbs.

The Bishop thinks that his friend needs the miraculous power of Christ applied to him. "You lack the power to believe," he says, "as though you lacked a member of your body or one of your senses. Your greatest fault is trying to reason yourself into belief." "What do I need to remedy my reason?" asks the writer. "A great suffering." "I have suffered." "A great love." "That I have known." "You are an incomprehensible man." "As all men are."

The triumphal entry, says the author, was a parable. "And do you recognize the Son of God in this rider on His lowly beast?" asks the Bishop. "I recognize Him, and with the children I shout hosannas and clap my hands." This dialogue ends with this conclusion to which the Bishop cannot but agree: Socrates, in spite of his death, and Plato, in spite of his doctrine, are two dialecticians of morals; Confucius is near Christ, not because of his life but because of his teachings, since he too has founded a religion, but his is a religion without mystery, without dynamic and without universality. The Master described the Kingdom of Heaven as an earthly realization, a state of grace of the soul. After twenty centuries humanity is still realizing this, in individuals by spiritual progress, and in the species by political progress. The enterprise is not finished, and there is coming into the world in these times a new mystic hope. Humanity goes distracted like the industrious Cleophas on the road to Emmaus at the twilight hour, and the Risen Christ comes in invisible form to give the soul of humanity a new message. The new message is like a song in the night and His doctrine is the simple doctrine of love.

The third and last dialogue, " The Spirit of Christ," takes us still higher in its Christian view of a far-reaching horizon, as seen from the height of the ideal of the spirit of the invisible Christ in the universe.

As in the first dialogue he utilized the best of all religions in the working out of his own salvation; here he weighs the good of all nations. It will be interesting to note his estimate of Christianity in the United States, which, he says, is Christian, the same as this Latin America is Christian.

" In the United States, a country of Protestant origin, formed by a cosmopolitan immigration, with freedom of worship, under whose protection live thousands of Buddhists and millions of Jews; a land of skyscrapers, jazz and picture shows; a land dizzy with mechanics and business and emancipated women, the Parliament passes temperance laws, the people consider riches as a predestination of grace and the rich donate their millions to social service, while the working-man works for a good salary during the week and reads his Bible on Sunday. The material life of the United States to me is either incomprehensible or absurd; but as to religious sentiment, there occur, as in all Saxon lands, such things as in our country would be impossible or ridiculous, and which balance material progress."

His estimate of the Roman Catholic Church is not deprecatory, but he points it to a higher mission. The Church, like the good shepherd, should gather to itself the sheep outside the Church. The Bishop is firm in saying that the Church has the custody of the flock and, if they do not believe in the Church, they are to be left outside. In speaking of the Church the writer says: " I do not deny that the hearth fire might again glow, but the ashes are without light and heat. I do not refer to the indifferent or lukewarm, but rather to the masses of the faithful, when I say that there has never been an honest mental anxiety over the religious problem, which is a grave fault for a newly-born culture. Such anxiety, if it existed, might give to politics a moral content."

In Confucius and other oriental founders of religion he sees a Chinese Christ, with their own Bible, their own Bethlehem star, their own triumphal entry. In all these lands there exists the spirit of the invisible Christ, or the longing for Him. Jesus, when on earth, spoke more of life than of death. Life was an earthly reality as much as an existence after death. " The only prayer that Jesus taught His disciples does not ask that we may go to His Kingdom but that His Kingdom come to us." " You look at Christ from the height of your cathedral, I feel Him in the depth of my soul. I feel the invisible Church of souls, in which the Master presides, and in which each should commune with the spirit of Christ."

The great need of the present-day Church is a spiritual revival. Since, and owing to, the last war and to the present-day crisis, the Church of Rome is obliged to assume a creative attitude, as it has done in other critical times. The world needs a fresh coming of the Messiah, not a physical coming but a spiritual. Where shall this revival take place ? The Bishop weighs the possibilities. China, he says, with its obscure cloisters ; India, with its immutable castes ; Israel, with the Messiah excluded ; cannot be the initiators of a new Christian realization. Europe with its lack of spiritual unity is not the place for it ; Islam, with its fanaticism overthrown, still less. Nor can it be in the United States with its capitalistic imperialism, nor in Japan with its Westernized industrialism and militarism. The author sees in the Argentine the land predestined to be the scene of this new and greater Christian awakening. His reasons for thinking so are that there is plenty of room, there is a true democracy, all men are brothers, there is a great future in every way.

Early in this series of dialogues the Bishop asks the author if he is a Roman Catholic. He answers that he was born in a Roman Catholic family and baptized a Roman Catholic, by the wish of his parents. Later he asks if he is a Protestant. He answers that he is not. The Bishop seems to think that he appears to be one at times. When he quotes from a book on theosophy, the Bishop asks if he is a theosophist. He answers that he is not. Then what is he ? " If you wish to put me under some denomination," he declares, " you may call me a Christian. I am a Christian by lineage and sentiment. I recognize in each man a brother, be he Roman Catholic, Protestant or Buddhist, or of whatever profession. There you have my definition short and simple." " Short, yes," answers the Bishop, " but not simple." " Christ is my religion," answers the author, " and His Gospel is my law."

The above somewhat lengthy quotation is of immense value as showing the attitude of a cultured Latin American who has maintained or cultivated a warm Christian faith, but, because of the Church's failure to come up to his high ideals, cannot find a spiritual home in the Roman Catholic Church, and, probably because of his inborn suspicion of Protestantism, carefully instilled during his boyhood by priests and relations, cannot hold communion with this Church of the Reformation. He nobly professes his faith in Christ, but, due to circumstances over which he has no control, feels that he must remain churchless and without that help and inspiration which would come to him from contact with a community of believers, and thus seeks to maintain within himself that warm Christian fervour which could be of inestimable benefit if communicated to others. His Christ is the " Invisible Christ," disassociated from the churches, who needs no temple and no ritual, no intercessory priest, but who speaks directly to the heart of every individual. This is a conception which will appeal to many cultured Latin Americans who are suspicious of the only Church they have known. The book is destined to have a wide influence among its readers.

(*d*) The Opinion of Viscount Bryce.

One other writer must be quoted here, and in this case no less an authority than Viscount Bryce, who made a careful study of social and religious conditions on the occasion of his visit in 1912.

In his carefully written report, referring to the situation as he had found it, he wrote :

" Another fact strikes the traveller with surprise. Both the intellectual life and the ethical standards of conduct of these countries seem to be entirely divorced from religion. The women are almost universally ' practising Catholics,' and so are the peasantry, though the Christianity of the Indians bears only a distant resemblance to that of Europe. But men of the upper or educated class appear wholly indifferent to theology and Christian worship. It has no interest for them. They are seldom actively hostile to Christianity, much less are they offensive when they speak of it, but they think it does not concern them, and may be left to women and peasants. . . .

" In the more advanced parts of South America (this would refer to the region studied in this book), it (the Church) seems to be regarded as a harmless Old World affair, which belongs to a past order of things just as much as does the rule of Spain, but which may, so long as it does not interfere with politics, be treated with the respect which its antiquity commands. In both cases the undue stress laid upon the dogmatic side of theology and the formal or external side of worship has resulted in the loss of spiritual influence. In all the Spanish countries, the Church has trodden down the laity and taken freedom and responsibility from them more than from anywhere else in Christendom, making devotion consist in absolute submission. Thus, when at last her sway vanished, her moral influence vanished with it. This absence of a religious foundation for thought and conduct is a grave misfortune for Latin America."*

---

* James Bryce, *South America, Observations and Impressions,* p. 582.

III.

The Coming of the Evangelical Missions
Their Work and Problems

WITH this somewhat sombre background as a setting, and with the political and economic unrest which prevailed in South America about one hundred years ago, the evangelical forces of Great Britain and the United States of America first awoke to their spiritual responsibilities to the country. Plans were accordingly projected for work throughout this region among people altogether under the rule of the Church of Rome.

Since the young republics had but recently broken the ties that bound them to Spain, and were busy in organizing and settling up independent Governments, the time was propitious for the introduction of new ideas : but authority was not yet centralized, and, instead of an actual republic, authority in all this region was exercised by military dictators, each of whom ruled over a certain section or group of the people. This, however, was but the first step in the evolution toward real democracy. The leaders of the time were particularly noted for their willingness to entertain new ideas from abroad. In the early years of the century, this was true, even as regards the clergy. Fired by a desire for liberty, even in church matters, the clergy were a source of anxiety to the ecclesiastical authorities in Rome, who through them desired to impose their will upon the people, but were hindered by the slow communications of the times.

Mention should be made of a few of the outstanding pioneers and the work that has grown from their labours.

1. *J*

T
as in
man
Lancaste...
great progress in
Joseph Lancaster, its
Foreign School Society, which
carry forward its programme, decid
introduce the system in South America.
outstanding features of the system was the
use of leaves from the Bible for instructing the
in reading, this being in accordance with an arrange
ment made by Joseph Lancaster with His Majesty,
King George III. James Thomson was chosen as
the one who should attempt to introduce the system
into South America, which was known to be education-
ally needy, as well as politically and spiritually in a
somewhat chaotic condition. He brought also the
representation of the British and Foreign Bible Society.
In a somewhat naïve volume of *Letters,** published
in 1827, of which but few copies are now extant, he
tells us that he reached Buenos Aires on October 6th,
1818, after a voyage from Liverpool of twelve weeks
and three days, and at once made proposals to the
Government in Buenos Aires regarding the introduction of the Lancasterian system of education. He
was well received, even by some of the clergy of the
Church of Rome, and was given every facility to
inaugurate and carry on his work, while the Government authorities continued to be his friends and
helpers during the three years of his residence in or
near the capital.

On leaving the country, he reported that a number
of schools had been founded in various parts of Argentina and in Montevideo, with a total of five thousand
pupils, and that he had also been successful in distributing large numbers of the Bible. In recognition

---

* *Letters on the Moral and Religious State of South America*, by James
Thomson. Published by James Nesbit, London.

...fore leaving for Chile,
...Republic and given very
...resident and other officials
...was strongly urged to remain
...uguay, where he was offered a
...n the schools, but felt compelled
...rney to the countries of the west
...again met with great success.

...hind him well organized evangelical
...a fully developed programme for their
...ce : but well-trained teachers were lacking,
...ove all, the evangelical community in Great
...ain had not fully awakened to its opportunity.
As it happened, these schools languished and died.
Had well-prepared, consecrated men and women been
sent out in sufficient numbers to carry on the work
begun by Thomson, the religious history of this region,
and of all South America, during the past century
would have been a very different one.

A President of the University of Chile, referring
to Thomson and his work, has called it the " Golden
Age of Protestantism in South America," evidently
meaning that a great and unusual opportunity was
lost by those who should have taken advantage of it,
and that the same possibilities would not again occur.

2. *Allen F. Gardiner, Apostle to the Indians.*

The next great single figure in the establishment
of evangelical Christianity in South America is that
of Captain Allen F. Gardiner, R.N., the first evangelical
Christian, so far as we know, to become interested in
the Indians of this continent. This interest was first
aroused during a visit paid by him to Chile, in 1822,
in a vessel of His Majesty's fleet. His work for South
America may be considered as dating from that year,
but it was not until sixteen years later that he was
able to free himself entirely from other responsibilities
and undertake his missionary labours. The next ten
years were spent in fruitless attempts to establish
work, first in Chile, afterwards in Bolivia, and then

in Argentina.   Finally, in 1850, he succeeded in organizing an expedition, and with six companions sailed for Tierra del Fuego, on September 27th of that same year.   In December they were put ashore in Banner Cove in the Straits of Magellan, and their vessel, the " Ocean Queen," went on its way to the west coast ports.

The history of the attempt from this time on spells tragedy.   Provisions had been taken for six months and arrangements made for a second supply to leave England not later than March, 1851.   But there were unexpected and, it seems, unavoidable delays, and when the rescuing party finally reached Earnest Cove in Spaniard Harbour, in September, 1851, it was to find that the entire party of seven had succumbed to disease and starvation some twenty days before.   Gardiner's last written words were : " I trust that poor Fuegia and South America may not be abandoned " ; and " If I have a wish for the good of my fellow men, it is that the Tierra del Fuego Mission might be prosecuted with vigour, and the work in South America commenced."

The Mission in England had no thought of abandoning the work.   Another expedition was at once organized, and fitted out, and despatched.   It seemed at first that great progress was being made in securing the confidence of the natives, but on Sunday, November 6th, 1859, at Woolya, Navarin Island, the entire party save the cook, who remained on board the vessel, were suddenly set upon by the natives and slaughtered while conducting public worship on shore.   The whole Mission was thus blotted out and the outlook was such as would have discouraged any missionary society.

But although these early attempts to evangelize the Indians of South America were, humanly speaking, a tragic failure, yet the heroic death of Captain Gardiner, and later of the group at Woolya, only served to awaken still greater interest in the work to which they had given their lives.   This but strengthened the usual British determination to carry on, and the South American Missionary Society, in spite of financial limitations and lack of workers to enter this difficult field has, even till now, loyally endeavoured to carry forward the work of its founder.   Its present-day activities will be dealt with later.

3.   *The Presbyterians from the U.S.A.*

The Board of Foreign Missions of the Presbyterian Church in the United States of America was the first of the great Missionary Boards of North America to attempt to establish its work in this region.   The breaking away from Spain and the setting up of republican forms of Government by the people of South America, but especially the close copying of the Constitution of the United States by Argentina and other youthful nationalities, had awakened deep interest and sympathy among the people of the older Republic to the north.   There was in particular a feeling that the time was ripe for the offering of spiritual help, and a number of the Boards reached the point of discussing the extension of their work to this region. But, in spite of the fact that the missionary spirit among the evangelical Churches was not yet strongly developed, that the Boards themselves were but recently organized and were financially weak, and that few candidates were offering themselves for work abroad, the Board of Foreign Missions of the Presbyterian Church in the United States of America decided to open work in Buenos Aires.   In April, 1826, the Rev. Theophilus Parvin, its first missionary, reached that city.   He had been ordained by the Presbytery of Philadelphia and, although sent out by the Board, came with the intention of establishing a self-supporting work.   He soon obtained a position as a teacher, and later was appointed Professor of Greek and English in the University of Buenos Aires.   This position he eventually resigned and founded an Academy for boys, and subsequently opened another for girls.

Events seem to have moved swiftly, for in about a year the Mission was closed and the missionaries returned to the States.

Another attempt was made, in 1854, but the missionary appointed soon after took a position in a school, and in 1859 the Board definitely abandoned the enterprise. Any work which had been accomplished was taken over and carried on by the Scots Presbyterian Church. This Church is now the sole representative of Presbyterianism in this region.

4. *The Methodist Episcopal Church.*

Meanwhile, the Methodist Episcopal Board in the United States of America had become interested in this field, and in 1835 sent out the Rev. Fountain E. Pitts to examine the situation and report. As a result of his recommendations, in 1836, the Rev. Justin Spaulding and the Rev. John Dempster were sent out and immediately began work. Others arrived soon after to join these men and work was begun in Montevideo, as well as in Buenos Aires. But the Board soon found itself in serious financial difficulties and, near the end of 1841, was obliged to recall the missionaries and to close the Mission. This situation, however, was but temporary. In 1843, the Church in Buenos Aires was reopened by one of the missionaries who had been recalled, and the work has since then been continuous. To-day, as regards numbers and influence, it ranks first among the distinctly evangelizing groups of the region.

5. *The Baptists.*

The work of the Southern Baptists in this region was formally begun in 1903, but there were already a number of Baptist congregations in Argentina. Probably the first to organize their churches were immigrants from the German-speaking colonies of the Volga region in Russia, who arrived in 1877 and settled in the Province of Entre Rios. Among them were a number of Stundists of " Tanzbrüder," who organized meetings among the farming communities of the Province. They were occasionally visited by ministers from other groups, especially from the great German colony in the State of Rio Grande do Sul, in Brazil. Many of these congregations still exist and carry on work.

A French-speaking colony of Baptists in the Province of Santa Fé also maintained its services, and in 1881 the Rev. Paul Besson, a French Swiss pastor, in answer to their call took charge of the work. He suffered a great deal of persecution because of his activities, once being imprisoned. Transferring his work to Buenos Aires, he continued his agitation in favour of civil registries, and was largely instrumental in securing for the country this needed reform.

The first representative of the Southern Baptist Convention of the United States of America was the Rev. S. M. Sowell, who arrived in 1903. Both he and Mr. Besson are still active in the evangelical work of the region.

6. *The Disciples of Christ.*

The work of the Disciples was begun in Buenos Aires in 1906 and, under an arrangement for co-operation, they entered Paraguay about ten years later. This allowed the Methodist Mission to withdraw its workers permanently and centre its efforts more thoroughly in Argentina and Uruguay. The Disciples have no work outside Buenos Aires and Asunción, and in both these cities they give much of their attention to school work. In Buenos Aires they co-operate with the Methodist Mission.

7. *Other Groups.*

There are too many other evangelical groups carrying on work in this region to be described here in detail.* Their object is the evangelization of the native population. Some of these groups, though small, are doing a good work which is destined to

---

*A more complete list will be found in Appendix A, p. 119. For an account of those Societies working among the Indians, see p. 110.

grow in importance in the coming years. Others are not only weak in numbers and resources, but represent exotic tendencies which confuse the mind of the people whom they are striving to serve, and hold up to public scorn the manifold divisions of Protestantism. Many of the groups, however, are actuated by a spirit of brotherhood and co-operation, and gladly work with others in the larger interests of the Kingdom.

8. *Racial Groups.*

Various racial groups maintain their own churches, and, although in general they do not attempt direct evangelization of the native population, they are nevertheless a direct help in that they stand as representatives of the non-Roman Catholic forces, and are generally ready to co-operate with all other groups in matters of common interest and responsibility.

(*a*) The Anglican Church is easily first among such groups as it was the first on the field. It held its first service in Buenos Aires in 1824, and the first church building was opened in 1831. The first chaplain reached Buenos Aires in 1837, but services had been conducted by laymen prior to his arrival. The first building erected for a church was completed and dedicated in 1858.

One of the outstanding figures in the history of the work of this Church in Argentina is that of Bishop Stirling, who came out in priest's orders in 1860, as a forlorn hope—" God's lonely sentinel " he calls himself—to revive and carry on the work begun by Allen Gardiner. He lived among the Indians, and gained their confidence to such a degree that it was possible to reorganize and carry on the work which seemed to have been destroyed by the death of Captain Gardiner and his party. He was anointed Bishop of the Falkland Islands in Westminster Abbey in 1869, and served until 1909. After an interval of two years he was succeeded by the Right Rev. E. F. Every, D.D., who, since 1910, had been Bishop of the diocese of Argentina and Eastern South America. The centre of all Anglican work in this region is St. John's Pro-Cathedral, in Buenos Aires.

The Anglican Church carries on work other than that which directly concerns the spiritual care of the members of its own communion through the South American Missionary Society. It was founded at Brighton in 1844 as " The Patagonian Mission," with the object of promoting work in Patagonia, and its first Secretary was Captain Allen F. Gardiner, R.N. The present name was assumed in 1864. Its most important work has been among the Indians of the interior of Argentina and Paraguay, of which a fuller statement will be made elsewhere.*

One of its missionaries, the Rev. W. C. Morris, carries on a unique educational work in Palermo, a suburb of Buenos Aires. These schools were founded some thirty years ago as a distinctly evangelical venture, but, in order to exercise a wider influence and secure more generous public support, they were organized as a national institution, and adopted the name "Argentine Philanthropic Schools and Institutes." These schools reach many of the poorest children of the great city of Buenos Aires who might otherwise be left without schooling, and have an annual enrolment of over six thousand. There are now fifteen schools in the group. They are maintained by voluntary contributions, and both the national Government and the Municipality of Buenos Aires have contributed generously to their support. In many cases the influence of the school so affects the home that the entire family is lifted to a higher standard of living. Since their foundation thousands of children have been prepared for active and helpful participation in business and industrial life, and thus have become useful citizens.

The Society also maintains the " Allen Gardiner Homes " for orphans or poor children of English-speaking parents, near Córdoba, and a " Children's Home " in Belgrano, a suburb of Buenos Aires.

---

* See p. 110.

There are also a number of very fine British schools in or near Buenos Aires which are, at least indirectly, under the direction of the Bishop of this diocese, the chief one being St. George's College for Boys, at Quilmes.

(*b*) The first general meeting of the Scots Presbyterians resident in Argentina was called in 1828 for the purpose of securing the services of a minister of the Church of Scotland. The Rev. William Brown, who was already on the field as minister of an independent congregation, was called, and he accepted the position. The first services were held in a room in the minister's house on March 14th, 1829.

From this small beginning the work has steadily grown to its present important position in the community. The St. Andrew's Scots Church building is one of the finest Protestant church edifices in Latin America. The minister has a number of assistants, generally young men fresh from the Scottish universities, among them one who gives his whole time to the scattered families and groups in the country towns and districts of Argentina and Uruguay, and another, a Spaniard, who is in charge of the important work among the Spanish-speaking community. There are several branch congregations in or near Buenos Aires, each with its own church building and equipment. These are served by the minister and his assistants from the central church. There is also a strong, well-endowed Scottish school which does an important work in the community, especially in providing a thorough education for children of Scottish ancestry who would otherwise be unable to receive an English education.

(*c*) The German Evangelical Church has an extensive work in both Buenos Aires and Montevideo. In each city it maintains a substantial church building, and also cares for its own people scattered throughout the three Republics. Congregations are maintained in many places outside the capital cities, and the Church has been a real and helpful influence in the life of the German community. It will be noted that the Church in Buenos Aires, as shown in the table given in Appendix D, has a membership of twelve thousand. This figure, no doubt, includes all its baptized members in this city and its environs. Social activities are also maintained by the German community, especially athletic fields and clubs. The standing of the German people is very high in these Republics. They make valuable colonists and take good care of their own nationals should they arrive in the country in needy circumstances.

(*d*) Another interesting colony is that of the Welsh in the Chubut Valley in Argentina in the Territory of Chubut, a district otherwise unoccupied save by a few representatives of the Anglican Church, who look after their own church people and schools. This colony was founded in 1866, when a hundred and fifty Welsh people settled in what was then a bleak and uninhabited land, with the desire to establish a new Wales in this corner of Patagonia. They suffered many disasters and hardships during the first years of their occupancy, but they held on and prospered to such an extent that they founded another colony nearer the Andes. The original colony occupies an alluvial plain, some five by forty miles in extent, through which the Chubut River flows eastward into the sea.

A number of these people migrated to Canada about twenty-five years ago, thus reversing the trek of the Mennonites.* A number of people of Latin nationality have moved into Chubut Valley, so that the country is no longer predominantly Welsh. This introduction of new blood has been a blessing, since the colony had suffered a certain degree of degeneracy through continued intermarriage. The present tendency is for the Welsh colonists to sell their farms and return to lands under the British flag. Many have found their way to Australia and to the United Kingdom.

---

* See p. 59.

In this Valley the Welsh have maintained their own churches and manifest their usual religious fervour. The Church of England has cared for its own people among them by establishing a chaplaincy at Trelew, the commercial capital of the Territory ; from this centre the chaplain serves a wide area.

(e) Inasmuch as the group making up the Mennonites in Paraguay represents one of the most ideal-impelled migrations on record, more than passing mention must be made of them in this Survey.

These people trekked from the cold prairies of Western Canada to the tropical plains of Paraguay, and have established their homes under totally new conditions. Their coming has been heralded locally as the greatest event of the kind since the Pilgrim Fathers boarded the Mayflower at Delft Haven.

The Company, which was formed for the purpose of transferring this colony to its new quarters and for making proper arrangements for its future development, secured from the Paraguayan Government a tract of land of some three million acres in extent, lying on the eastern slopes of the Andes and along the Paraguay river. This land is said to be ideally located and unusually fertile, and forms a part of an estate of seven million acres which originally belonged to one of the old families of Paraguay. Their neighbours are the wild Indians of the region, few in number and kept to their own reservations by a small force of Paraguayan soldiers furnished by the Government. This guard is made necessary because of the Mennonites' principles of non-resistance. Since these Indians are not warlike but are inclined to thieving, the function of the guard will be chiefly to protect property rather than life.

For several years representatives of the Mennonites studied the situation, and a charter was finally granted by the Paraguayan Government, which is so unusual that it deserves to be known to the world outside. According to its clauses the Mennonites are granted considerations, in accordance with their religious beliefs, which they have not been able to obtain elsewhere, such as exemption from military service, the right to conduct their own schools and churches in their own language, freedom from taking an oath, and the absolute control of the colony by their own representatives.

The charter was granted by a special law enacted for the purpose, and its main points are as under :

" ARTICLE I.   Members of the community known as Mennonites who come to the country as components of a colonization enterprise, and their descendants, shall enjoy the following rights and privileges :

" 1.   To practise their religion and to worship with absolute liberty without any restriction and, consequently, to make affirmation by a simple ' Yes ' or ' No ' in courts of justice, instead of by oath ; and to be exempt from obligatory service either as combatants or non-combatants, both in times of peace and during war.

" 2.   To establish, maintain, and administer schools and establishments of learning, and to teach and learn their language, which is German, without any restriction.

" ARTICLE II.   The sale of alcoholic or intoxicating beverages is prohibited within a zone of five kilometres from the properties belonging to the Mennonite colonies, unless the competent authorities of these colonies request the

Government to permit such sale and the Government accedes to the request.

" ARTICLE III. The following concessions are granted to the Mennonite colonies for a period of ten years from the arrival of the first colonists :

" 1. The free entry of furniture, machinery, utensils, drugs, seeds, animals, implements, and, in general, of everything that may be necessary for the installation and development of the colonies.

" 2. Exemption from all classes of national and municipal taxes.

" ARTICLE IV. No immigration law, or law of any other character, existing or that may be passed in future, shall impede the entrance of Mennonite immigrants into the country because of their age or physical or mental incapacity."

The Mennonites are known to be an earnest, hard-working, practical-minded, religious people, and their venture will be watched with sympathetic interest.

From a missionary standpoint this migration may have far-reaching consequences. The presence in Paraguay of such a large number of Protestant Christians, whose customs and religious habits are so entirely different from those of the Roman Catholic population of the country, must inevitably influence the Government and the people with whom they come into contact.

The section of the country to which they go is far removed from the capital, and they will be surrounded by Indians, who have heretofore been considered hostile to all attempts to reach them with civilization.

Although the Mennonites have reached this Promised Land with no definite missionary motive, their very presence should arouse questions among their neighbours ; and is it not conceivable that the spirit of investigation, having once been aroused, will work wonders, and help to bring about a change in a country dominated by ecclesiastics for centuries?

(f) The Boers from South Africa also form an interesting group in the Territory of Chubut, Argentina. After the war with Great Britain, which ended in the defeat of the Boer forces and the loss of their nationality, a number of families left South Africa and came to Southern Argentina, where they secured grants of land from the Government. The first families arrived in 1902, and about 1905 a specially chartered vessel brought two hundred colonists who settled in the southern part of the Territory of Chubut, forming a colony known as Escalante. The number has fluctuated by reason of new arrivals, and departures of old settlers. At the present time the colony consists of about eight hundred individuals. Many now live in the port, Comodoro Rivadavia, and some have moved to Buenos Aires and other cities and towns of the Republic.

A tract of sixty square leagues of land was granted to this colony, and many of the colonists, in spite of the initial difficulties, have developed their portions and have prospered.

(g) The Waldensians are one of the most homogeneous, influential and numerous of the evangelical groups in this region. The first immigrants from Italy arrived in 1856, and there has been a healthy growth of the colony, both by continued immigration and by natural increase, until there are now some twelve thousand in all.

The first colonists settled in Uruguay, where they were given land and certain concessions by the Government, and their principal centres are still in that Republic. But several thousand have overflowed into Argentina and have established churches.

These colonists have prospered and now form the most numerous group of Waldensians outside Italy. They have hitherto brought their ministers from the homeland, but there is at present considerable interest in developing a national ministry from among their young men who are Uruguayans or Argentines. Two students are now in the Union Theological Seminary of Buenos Aires. The missionary zeal of this group of Christians has not been great, but, in the midst of a population that at first was both intolerant and inclined to persecution, they have held their own people faithful to their religion. They are noted for their honesty and uprightness of life. Many of the younger generation occupy high positions in business and professional circles. The contribution made by these representatives of a Church that has for centuries withstood persecution, has been of very great import-ance to the progress and standing of evangelical Christianity in this region. There is reason to believe that in the years to come it will be greater.

(h) The Jews, while not included among the Christian groups, must be mentioned as forming an important non-Roman Catholic section of the community, and as caring for their own people in a religious sense. There is a steady influx of Israelites into Argentina, under the auspices of the Jewish Colonization Asso-ciation, whose centre is in Paris. The Director General of this Association is quoted as having recently stated :

" After thirty years of experience in Canada, Poland, Palestine, etc., we have become convinced that Israelites receive in no other part of the world the hospitable welcome and the promising results from their work that they receive in Argentina. The Association has already secured about 370,000 hectares (about 914,274 acres) of arable land in that country, and has a total property of 600,000 hectares (about 1,482,600 acres).

" The Zionist problem causes us no worry in Argentina, but this is not true of Poland, Palestine, and other countries, where the Israelite is forced to enter into a political and defensive struggle, while in

Argentina a cordial hospitality is extended to the Jews. This is true to such an extent that the Association urges its colonists to assimilate and identify themselves with the Argentine environment."*

Among the plans announced by the Association for the social betterment of its colonists is the securing of large sections of arable land in the vicinity of the great industrial centres, where the workman can take advantage of the time he has free from his labour to cultivate vegetables and fruits, and thus provide employment for himself and his family. To this end, negotiations are to be undertaken to acquire large plots of land in the vicinity of Santa Fé, Rosario, and other manufacturing centres, which will be divided into small lots for the use of the colonists.

There is at present no attempt being made by any Christian Church to give the Gospel to these Jews, and it is evident that the problem, due to the increased immigration of people of this race, will in time become of considerable importance.

In 1905, the latest year for which statistics have been issued by the Association, there were 33,135 Jews in Argentina who are or have been colonists. The centre of Jewish population is in Entre Rios. It should be noted that this figure does not represent the non-colonials arriving in the country. The total population in the three Republics reaches a considerably higher figure. Synagogues are maintained in a number of centres and serve as spiritual and social centres for the community.

(i) There are a number of other racial groups who maintain religious services among their own people, but whose communities are small as compared with those already mentioned. Their work, however, is most important and contributes greatly to the volume of Christian service in this region. Among these groups are the Armenians, who hold services regularly in one of the church buildings of another group in Buenos Aires, with one of their own nationality in charge.

---

* La Nación, Buenos Aires, February 6th, 1928.

The Danish community has its own pastor in Buenos Aires. The Dutch Reformed Church has a pastor whose work lies in Buenos Aires, and whose visits extend to groups near the city. The Swedish community maintains its own worship under its own pastor. The Orthodox Russian Church and the Orthodox Syrian Church also have their churches, each with their own pastor or priest.

Not one of these groups, so far as the writer has been able to learn, attempts any work outside its own colony in the capital of Argentina ; but, in view of the increasing number of immigrants from the countries they represent, many of whom go into the smaller towns of the interior, their work is destined to be of greater importance with each succeeding year.

9. *The Bible Societies.*

Chief among the interdenominational forces are the two Bible Societies, whose work is of the greatest benefit to all the groups of the region. Their agents and secretaries have been the forerunners of the missionaries and, as the work has progressed, their most valued and indispensable helpers. It would be impossible to calculate the good that has been done by these Societies since their entrance into this region. The number of copies of the Bible and portions that are sold increases from year to year.

There are numberless cases on record in which the Bible alone, without the aid of a missionary to interpret it, has been the direct means of intellectual enlightenment and spiritual conversion, both among representatives of the cultured classes as well as the proletariat. It stands before the community as embodying the essential principles of faith in Christ, which all Protestants accept in spite of their diverse organizations and seemingly conflicting creeds. One difficulty, of course, in the circulation of the Scriptures is the great extent of illiteracy, especially in country districts, and the consequent inability of the owner of a Bible to read it for himself.

E

As early as 1806 grants of the Scriptures were made to Spaniards in Buenos Aires, that is, four years before the Declaration of Independence. In 1811, the surprising statement was made that " priests in South America gratefully received a grant of Scriptures," and in 1813 some correspondence took place with a view to the establishment of work in the region of the Rio de la Plata. In this same year the Government issued a decree abolishing the Holy Office of the Inquisition.

As already noted, James Thomson visited Argentina and Uruguay in 1818, as a representative of the British and Foreign Bible Society. He was instrumental in making the Bible known and sold a large number of copies. The Society followed up his work by establishing an Auxiliary in 1822 and an Agency in 1825. Among its secretaries there have been many who were distinguished for their activities and daring in the circulation of the Scriptures. One of its notable secretaries in the '70 and '80 decades was Francis Neville Lett, sometime Anglican clergyman in Rosario, Santa Fé. The total circulation in the three Republics in 1925 through this Society was 111,283 copies, and these were offered in forty languages, the principal one, of course, being Spanish.

The La Plata Agency of the American Bible Society was established in 1864, and includes the Republics on the Rio de la Plata, and Chile. This Agency had for many years the services of the Rev. Francisco Penzotti, one of the most famous of all Bible agents in Latin America, and is now served, as secretary, by his son, the Rev. Paul Penzotti. The circulation of this Agency for 1925 was 134,300 volumes, and the total circulation in this region since the establishment of the Agency is 2,314,799 volumes.

10. *The Christian Associations.*

These two organizations, which are interdenominational in their work, and undenominational at the same time, have a wide field of influence in these great cities, and are making unusual progress.

The Young Men's Christian Association (Y.M.C.A.) was founded in Buenos Aires in 1902, and now has a membership of five thousand. There is an Association also in Montevideo, with eighteen hundred members and a new building which ranks as one of the finest of its kind in the world.

Plans are now under way for opening in Rosario and later in Asunción. The Association does active Christian work among both Roman Catholics and Protestants, and is a distinctive intellectual and spiritual force in the city and country. It has specialized in the care of delinquent and semi-delinquent boys, and has established homes or centres in which hundreds of these potential criminals are brought under reforming influences and sent out as useful members of society. One of its secretaries is now in charge of a Government Reformatory in which five hundred boys are being educated and cared for under the direction of this Christian man and his wife. Through its emphasis on athletics, the Association has done much to win the youth of the cities away from weakening diversions and to build up a strong virile manhood.

The Young Women's Christian Association (Y.W.C.A.) is carrying on a similar work for young women in Buenos Aires and Montevideo, though very much handicapped through lack of equipment and suitable buildings of its own. Plans are now under consideration for supplying this need which, when carried out, will put the Association into a position to do a much needed work among the young women of these great cities.

11. *School Work of the Evangelical Missions.*

Evangelical schools in this region are a comparatively modern venture of the various Missions— unlike the situation in Brazil and Chile, where a number of very important institutions were founded fifty or more years ago.

(a) Some of the most important schools.

The Methodists and Disciples of Christ co-operate

in the "American Grammar and High School and Ward Commercial Institute" in Buenos Aires. This school includes all grades from kindergarten to a complete secondary course which is officially affiliated with the school system of the Government. There are also separate courses in English for children of American and British parents who wish to complete their education in the homeland. There is a staff of some thirty masters, most of whom have been specially trained in national institutions. The six or eight American teachers, including the headmaster and his wife, are graduates of colleges and universities in the United States of America, and specially prepared for their work. There are about three hundred students in all departments.

Methodists, Disciples and Waldensians also co-operate in the Union Theological Seminary, which has five or six students, and the two first-named co-operate in the training school for women workers, which reports fifteen young women students.

A splendid site of some twenty acres just outside the city limits has recently been bought by these two co-operating bodies, and plans are being made to transfer the school and possibly the other institutions to this new location where they can be more intensively developed.

The Women's Board of Foreign Missions of the Methodist Church has a school for girls—"Crandon Institute"—in Montevideo, with about four hundred students and one of the finest educational buildings in South America. This Board also has a school for girls in Rosario, with a hundred and fifty students, in a good well-equipped building, and a school in this same city, known as "Gleason Institute" for poor children.

The Disciples of Christ have the "International College" in Asunción, and have recently erected two buildings which surpass all other school buildings in Paraguay, both as to size and internal equipment, and general suitability for teaching purposes. There are about a hundred and fifty pupils, both boys and girls, in this school.

The United Lutheran Church of the United States of America has an unusually successful school in Villa del Parque, a suburb of Buenos Aires. Although it was founded only ten years ago, it registers annually more than five hundred pupils. All grades are maintained, and there is a large staff of specially trained masters, the great majority of whom are Argentines.

The Southern Baptists have a school for boys and a theological seminary in Buenos Aires, the former with about seventy-five pupils and the latter with ten students.

The Methodist Mission also maintains a number of parochial schools in connection with its churches in the smaller towns and country districts, with probably five hundred pupils in all.*

(b) Reasons for maintaining these schools.

It would be very natural for the reader to enquire as to the necessity of establishing and maintaining these evangelical schools ; especially would this be the case in Argentina and Uruguay, where the percentage of illiterates is comparatively low and where, particularly in the capital and larger cities, the Governments energetically sustain a high grade school system with well prepared teachers and the most modern and complete equipment. The equipment of such schools always surpasses that of the Mission schools.

No doubt the real apologetic lies in the fact that the evangelical schools educate, while the Government institutions merely instruct. This distinction has been referred to already. According to law, in both Argentina and Uruguay, no religious instruction can be given in any school of the Government. This is a reaction against the former situation in which the Roman Catholic Church arrogated to herself and exercised the exclusive right to give such instruction, and the law which was made to exclude this Church from the schoolroom rightly excludes all others. Moreover, many of the teachers in the national schools are pronounced agnostics or atheists, and take care to

* The statistics of the evangelical schools of the three Republics will be found in Appendix B, p. 131.

inculcate these principles in their students.   They delight in proclaiming that science has explored the utmost depths of space and has found no God and no resting place for such a Being, and students are quick to accept such teaching as true and follow the lead of their instructors.

The writer of these pages, in a personal survey made some years ago in one of the professional schools of the university of a neighbouring republic, found that among the one hundred students one was a declared Evangelical, one stood as a faithful Roman Catholic, ten favoured the Evangelical faith, twenty favoured the Roman Catholic faith, the remainder were in open rebellion against or altogether indifferent to all religion.   This showed an unusually good percentage in favour of the Evangelicals, which was probably due to the fact that the one Evangelical was a student for the ministry and a young man of attractive personality.   The one listed as a Roman Catholic was a nephew of the local Bishop, which explained perhaps his loyalty to the Church.   The same, or similar percentages, might be found in other universities of this region, with the probability that a much smaller percentage would favour either Church.

Another writer, referring to the students in the University of Buenos Aires, writes :

" The National University at Buenos Aires has enrolled over four thousand young men of the influential classes of the Argentine Republic. At least half of them come from the smaller cities and towns and live in the boarding houses of the city.   The atmosphere in which these students live is not conducive to moral vigour.   There is every encouragement to immorality and gambling, which are the great vices, and unfortunately the great majority have no conscience on these sins.

" As regards religion, I would say that not over ten per cent. of them are more than nominally identified with Roman Catholicism, which is the State religion. Another ten per cent. take a hostile attitude towards the Roman Church. This hostility does not mean, however, that there is any sympathy with Protestantism, in the best sense of that word. They are in sympathy with a Protestantism that protests, but they have had no contact with evangelical Christianity. Christianity and Romanism, indeed, mean to them one and the same thing. The great mass of students are indifferent, never having given any thought to religious questions. They believe in nothing."

However, in spite of this sombre setting, there are students who recognize their need of moral instruction and lament its absence in the curricula. One such has recently voiced his regret in a public address delivered at the close of his course. He said :

" There is a universal profession, which is that of being a man. To be a man is the final end of every human creature. To form a man is the primary function of the university. And yet we, newly admitted to our profession, say farewell to these scenes of our labours in the classroom with the bitterness of spirit which comes from being obliged to confess that we have received no such instruction. Masters of a world of ideas, we are yet wandering in search of a moral ideal. In our march toward the Unknown, will our gross natural instincts be a sure guide ? Although we are to exercise a tremendous influence in our contact with others, our teachers have failed to point out to us the ethical end of our own personality. Thought is a force, a force that builds up or tears down. In order that ideas may have a constructive value, it is necessary that they have a healthy and solid orientation. For this I believe, and it is my most fervent desire, that the university should develop a more efficient programme in the moral education of youth. . . . The university, if it will but place virtue on an equality with science, will have done much to harmonize moral values and will have made its most splendid contribution to its graduates as they set out on the rough highway of life."*

---

* *La Mañana*, Montevideo, February 1st, 1921.

The evangelical schools attempt to give this religious instruction which is forbidden in those schools which work directly under the State. The Bible is generally used as a text-book, or in some cases is made optional. Small study groups are formed for the advanced students. Sunday schools are held for boarding students, and above all else the life of the Christian teacher is a powerful argument in favour of the power of true Christianity. The contact of life on life, even though no direct religious instruction be given, is a powerful influence for the breaking down of prejudices and the setting up of new ideals.

(c) Some of the results of the school work.

That which was written not long since to the President of Mackenzie College, in São Paulo, Brazil, might also be written to those in charge of the evangelical schools in this or any other region of Latin America. One who had been studying the influence of that college, unsolicited, wrote as follows:

" A great change has come over us here in São Paulo. We firmly believed that scientific thought and religious thought were incompatible or equally hostile. We have, however, found that religious thought is perfectly compatible with the most efficient scientific thought. You people at Mackenzie do not parade your religion, but you have it and make it felt and stand for it on any suitable occasion, and you are doing the best scientific training that is being done in Brazil to-day. For myself and many of my friends, I can say that we are convinced that the incompatibility of scientific thought is with a certain type of religious thought and not necessarily with Christianity. You can safely say to any intelligent audience in São Paulo to-day that God the Creator is the Governor from whom, by whom, and to whom all things pertain without exciting a sneer on the part of the thoughtful men."

The effort is to persuade students that the choice is not between education and religion, but that there is a possible alternative and that vital piety is not necessarily in conflict with knowledge.

Such schools also contribute to a better international understanding. Students who associate with foreign teachers, and are won by their personality as well as by their intellectual prowess, cannot fail to have a friendly feeling toward the land from which they come. In this way the schools also serve to prepare many students for study in foreign universities. Moreover, the children of the country in class-room and playing-field cannot fail to acquire a friendly feeling for the people among whom they were born or with whom they were compelled to spend a part of their childhood. In the same way that the Battle of Waterloo, according to the Iron Duke, was won on the playing-fields of Eton, so the struggle for a better understanding between nations may be brought measurably nearer to a successful conclusion by the mingling of the future citizens of the various republics in class-room and on athletic fields.

Pan-Americanism, which is too often declared to be but a dream of idealistic statesmen, can be brought about only through the production of a community of thought and ideals, and a single Christian school, planted and sustained by Anglo-Saxons in the midst of one of these Southern republics, is a finer and more effective gesture of goodwill and a far more effective agency for mutual understanding than many appeals that are more spectacular.

An Ambassador of the United States of America has recently written to the headmaster of one of the evangelical schools in Argentina, as follows :

"As you perhaps know, our regulations preclude me from making the public statements which I might in many cases be inclined to make. I am glad, however, to be able to tell you privately, after visiting your college on several occasions, and after seeing the type of work which you are doing—not only with American boys in the Argentine but with the youth of this country as well—your splendid staff of Argentine teachers and the prominent families represented in your student body, that as a medium of goodwill between the United States and Argentina I know of no similar organization or institution in Buenos Aires which is more promising in its future than the college which you so worthily represent."

Another, an official of the Government as Inspector of Secondary Education in the Republic, writes to the same headmaster, as follows :

" Being myself a promoter of American ways of life, I am very pleased with the fact that among our foreign private schools none has shown a more thorough and sympathetic understanding of its position before the Argentina society than the college under your principalship. Other European communities in Buenos Aires support splendid schools, with magnificent grounds and splendid buildings, but the ' Colegio Americano ' will always attract the parent who wishes a well balanced, intellectual, social and civic education for his son.

" Within its walls children of North American descent learn to love what is best in this country of ours ; while, on the other hand, our sons learn to discover the best side—so often hidden under the mass of sensational newspaper reports—of North American civilization and life. Frankly, I know no better means of cultivating international goodwill and mutual respect."

A physician of the city, an Argentine, who is also a professor in the college, writes :

" The ' Colegio Americano e Instituto Comercial Ward ' is not just another college added to those already in existence, but is a distinctive institution, with a definite mission completely new in our environment. Its moral ideals are especially new. It is an effort to link nations together, particularly North and South America, and offers a happy opportunity to impress upon the minds and hearts of the youth of the Argentine the beauty and truth of the Gospel without dogmas or sectarianism."

    (*d*) The attitude of the Roman Catholic Church toward Evangelical schools.

As to the opinion of these schools, held by the dominant Church, the following edict issued by the secretary of the Bishop in one of these three Republics will speak for itself. It reads as follows :

" Secretary's Office.

" To the parish priests and persons in charge of churches :

" By order of my superior, I communicate to you the following : that the administration of the . . . college has had printed and is circulating a prospectus of the teaching which is given in that institution, in the context of which are found certain declarations which amply confirm the judgment which it has always deserved from the time of its foundation, that if it is a centre of instruction, it is also and principally a centre of Protestant propaganda. Among other statements it is enough to cite the following by reason of their being very explicit.

" That the . . . college was founded under the auspices of the . . . society (a powerful organization, well known as an instrument of world-wide Protestant propaganda, located in the United States of America).

" We consider religion as a matter of living rather than as a thing of dogmas and rites.

" Not being able, therefore, to entertain a single doubt as to the completely Protestant character of the institution referred to, His Excellency, the Bishop, has ordered that the parish priests and persons in charge of public churches, from the first feast day and as many times as they may deem it necessary, invoking this order, shall advise the faithful that it is not lawful for them to send their children to the said school, nor to cooperate in any fashion with its anti-catholic ends.

" This notification will be grounded on the explanations necessary to the situation.

" (Signed) . . . Secretary."

An Editorial from the local Roman Catholic paper, commenting on the above edict, declares :

" We never tire of crying : ' The . . . College is Protestant ! ' Our zealous and vigilant Bishop and Pastor thus informs us that you must never for any reason or benefit, neither for its sumptuous meals, its magnificent North American furnishings, nor for any of its games and diversions which it offers as bait in order to ' fish ' souls, enrol your children in its luxurious palace of eternal perdition. It is our duty to advise those who are ignorant that they must not enter their children in such a school.   The parents of families who enrol their children in Protestant schools commit a mortal sin, and not even in the hour of death will they be able to receive the benefit of religion if they do not withdraw them beforehand from the above-mentioned institution."

Special care must be exercised, however, not to associate this school work with the political movement known as Pan-Americanism. This is a term that has lost immensely because of misuse by the politicians, and all Christian work in Latin America will do well to disassociate itself completely from this and all other political movements. Christian work must live and move and have its being in an entirely different sphere. This is particularly true at present, where there are such gross misunderstandings as to the policies of the great Republic of the North in its dealings with some of the weaker nationalities of the Western hemisphere, and where " Pan-Americanism " is the shibboleth so often invoked by local politicians as a shield behind which they may take refuge.

12. *Politics hinder Mission Work.*

It is an undoubted fact that the present political situation tends to make difficult all kinds of mission work in Latin America, and particularly in these Republics of the Rio de la Plata where, as in no other section, a national feeling has developed, and the latinization of all things is the goal of many of the most active politicians and social leaders. Anglo-Saxons are very often looked at askance and are heralded by these active national leaders as too cold and calculating to assimilate readily with the peoples of Latin blood and heritage. The dominant Church is all too willing to endorse this outlook and insist that while Protestantism may suit the Nordic temperament, it can never prevail among the people of Latin and hence Roman Catholic heritage, and must therefore be shunned.

It will be well, therefore, to keep mission work within its proper limits, with an absolute disassociation from political parties or pretensions. If this is true in the Orient, it is much more true in the Western world where we deal with modern and self-sufficient peoples who are especially jealous of their own prerogatives and look with suspicion on the foreigner. There is a tendency to look upon Protestantism as something distinctly Anglo-Saxon. It is important then that the presentation of Christianity should be kept free from such misunderstandings as may so easily arise from racial and political complications.

IV.

Some Special Problems before the Evangelical Church

1. *The Development of National Leadership.*

No doubt the greatest problem before the evangelical forces to-day is the preparation of efficient national leaders who will carry on the work begun, and until the present very largely conducted, by foreigners. In the past years there has been a deplorable tendency to accept as candidates for the ministry young men whose most pronounced and only recommendation was their willingness to serve. Very few of these had received the benefit of a serious course of study, and, after a short preparation in the special tenets of this or that Church group, they were sent out as fully authorized ministers of the Gospel. To-day, there is fortunately a determination to exact a much more complete scholastic preparation on the part of those entering on theological studies. In this way the tone of the evangelical national ministry will in time be raised.

The Union Seminary of Buenos Aires now demands the completion of the full secondary course of studies in a Government school, or its equivalent. Other seminaries have not advanced so far, but are gradually raising their entrance requirements.

The clamant need for an increase in the number of national ministers may be deduced from some of the statistics given. The Methodist Episcopal Church Conference, for example, the strongest in this region, reports a net gain of only four ordained ministers in ten years, or twelve in thirty-four years ; the figures in this case include both national and foreign workers. At the present time there are three students in the

Seminary.   The Disciples of Christ after more than twenty years of work in this region, with a special responsibility for the entire Republic of Paraguay and three great Argentine provinces, have but three national ministers and no students in the Seminary. The Waldensians have two students in the Union Seminary in Buenos Aires.   The Southern Baptists report ten students, and some of the smaller and interdenominational groups, which specialize in evangelistic work but do not stress a higher scholastic preparation, have a limited number in Bible Institutes or otherwise under instruction. Since these are the most active of the professedly missionary groups, it is evident that unless there is larger success in attracting capable leaders evangelical work is in danger of disappearing from the field. The foreigner must decrease as in Mexico, and as this will happen rapidly unless there is an increase of national helpers the work of past years will be sacrificed and progress made impossible in the future.

It is possible, as has happened in other fields, even in Latin America, that the inevitable withdrawal of the foreign element might bring to the surface and develop latent talent in the national evangelical forces. This would prove a blessing in disguise.   Leading Nationalists do not admit that the time has come for such withdrawal. A more united effort to raise up native leaders seems to be demanded.

2. *The Development of the Social Implications of Christianity.*

The work of the Evangelical Churches in this region, as in all Latin America, has been largely limited to evangelistic endeavour.   Schools are but a recent addition to their work.   The social side of Christianity as represented by hospitals, orphanages, medical help, etc., has been very generally neglected. There is no evangelical hospital in either of the capital cities, save a small one under the Salvation Army in Buenos Aires.   The Seventh-Day Adventists have a

sanatorium in the interior of Argentina, but there is
no institution of this kind in either Paraguay or
Uruguay. It is true that they are not an urgent necessity in the large cities, but they are greatly needed in
the smaller towns and country districts.

The establishment of evangelical hospitals and
other medical work under foreign Christian physicians
has been retarded if not made almost impossible by
the laws which forbid the practice of medicine by
foreigners. The revalidation of diplomas, while theo-
retically possible, is in practice so fraught with
difficulties as to be practically impossible. Unfortunately, there are as yet but few national physicians
among the evangelical community who are interested
in this altruistic use of their profession.

3.   *The Production of Good Literature.*

The preparation and distribution of clean literature
is one of the real problems before the Evangelical
Churches. Much that is sold at the news-stands and
even in the bookstores is of a salacious, pornographic
character, and much of that which is not distinctly
unclean is of an erotic type, patterned after a certain
class of French writers, and unsuited for general
circulation. Good books for the young people are
especially lacking, as also literature that will aid
evangelization.

To meet this need, at least in part, a Union Evangelical Bookstore has been organized in a central
position in Buenos Aires, under the title "La Aurora",
and has met with much success. Five different
organizations have united in forming this company—
the Methodist Episcopal, the Disciples of Christ, the
Scots Presbyterian, the Young Women's Christian
Association and the Religious Tract Society of London.
A number of individuals have also taken shares.

This Society proposes, so far as its resources will
permit, to help in the creation of Christian literature,
and at the same time to specialize in securing and
offering for sale the best books in all classes of literature.

4. *Co-operation.*

The problem of securing co-operation between the various groups, without in any way lessening their individual activities or detracting from denominational loyalty, is being managed by a local Committee on Co-operation, a branch of the general Committee on Co-operation in Latin America, whose offices are in New York. This Committee is well organized, with official representatives from most of the leading groups. It maintains an office and an executive secretary, and takes the lead in the organization of inter-denominational activities within the three Republics. There is a friendly feeling among the co-operating groups which has a helpful influence, even on the non-co-operating groups.

5. *A Union Hymnbook.*

The preparation of a Union Hymnbook that will meet the needs of a majority of the groups has long been a subject of discussion, and now, through the offices of the Committee on Co-operation in Latin America, seems to be nearing a solution. A special sub-Committee has been at work for a number of years selecting hymns through consultation with the musical leaders of the various groups. A selection has been made which, it is hoped, will be used by the various Church organizations.

6. *Nationalism.*

The rapidly growing spirit of nationalism creates a problem which threatens the very existence of the evangelical work. With a ministry that is inadequate, both numerically and by training, and with insufficient financial resources, the native Church is not yet in a position to declare its independence of Mission Boards. Some of the more advanced national leaders do not as yet understand that self-government must be based on self-support and self-propagation ; notwith-

F

standing they are anxious to assume control, elect a Bishop or other leaders from their own number, and constitute themselves a purely national organization. But, although this tendency is for many reasons to be encouraged, the Nationalists must yet realize the necessity of an increasing emphasis on self-support, rather than the cultivation of eloquence expended in presenting the glories of, and the benefits to be derived from, self-direction.

It must be admitted that the inability of the nationals to understand the necessity of a more generous support of the work is due, in some cases, to the teaching of some of the early leaders who emphasized, to an unwarranted degree, that salvation is a gift " without money and without price," as distinguished from the teaching of the dominant Church, in which nothing is free. The presence of foreign money has, no doubt, built up a kind of dependency on such aid, and it may take years to educate the national Churches to throw away this crutch and walk alone. It is only fair to remember that the membership con- sists almost entirely of men and women from the humbler walks of life, who possess little of this world's goods.

The example set by Mexico in allowing only nationals to exercise the rights of clergymen has had a widespread effect in other Latin American countries, and the ideal of Hispano-American solidarity, so ardently advocated by a few political and literary leaders, serves to keep alive the idea of nationalization. Much patience will be needed on both sides to keep a proper balance in this matter, and which, while con- serving what has been gained through much sacrifice in the past, will keep pace with the altogether legitimate desire of our national brethren to assume entire re- sponsibility for and control of the work. One missionary organization in this region has already voted to bring no more foreign missionaries to the field, save for special appointments such as to schools, theological seminaries, etc.

7.   *Relations with the Dominant Church.*

Undoubtedly, one of the most difficult questions before the Evangelical Church is that of the relation to be sustained with the forces of the dominant Church, and the proper method of approach by Protestantism to Roman Catholicism.   While the evangelical forces are not, in general, endeavouring to proselytize among the members of the Roman Catholic Church, yet it is impossible, in view of the immense majority of at least nominal adherents of that Church in the population, to avoid coming into contact and sometimes into conflict with its hierarchy.   What should be the attitude of the evangelical worker in such circumstances ?

The writer believes that there should be, above all else, an attitude of friendliness towards the representatives of the Roman Church, an effort to understand and appreciate the difficulties under which they work, and a spirit of willingness to co-operate with that Church in the solution of the problems of the day. This spirit may not be appreciated, but nevertheless it should exist.   The evangelical missionary cannot lay claim to omniscience, nor has he a monopoly of sanctity.   Moreover, whatever may be the faults of the Church of Rome, it was here maintaining the doctrines of the Cross, in its own way, for some three hundred years before the evangelical forces began to awaken to their responsibility.   If co-operation and mutual respect can be brought about in commerce and along political lines, it should be possible to bring them about also in other directions.

A business man of high standing in the United States of America, referring to this question, has recently written :

" Co-operation in its truest and best form is fundamentally important in producing the proper measure of success.   In South and Central American countries, we find a different people.   In the light of previous experience, I do not feel that our efforts will be successful if we endeavour to force upon our Southern neighbours our ideas of education and of religion and creed ; but I am sure that we can help reciprocally in promoting the religious and educational conditions in those countries, and in bringing about a more thorough understanding of the aspirations of each. We have much to learn, as well as to teach, and our efforts in any direction will not be properly productive if we do not learn this lesson. Through a proper recognition of this, we shall be able to gain the confidence of the South American nations, and promote moral values and national and personal ideals."

The missionary in South America to-day, however, meets a situation similar to that in the Philippines, which was described by a Roman Catholic priest in these words : " An appalling spirit of religious indifference is settling upon the rising generation, which is growing up without religion and without God. . . . Unless mighty efforts are now made to save the country, it will degenerate into a godless and atheistic land."

His message must be free from politics since, as a foreigner, he can have no part in the political life of the country, and yet he can make it clear that evangelical Christianity has no quarrel with true democracy, but is at once its source and most ardent supporter.

The mystical side of Christianity has been emphasized during all these centuries, and has not produced satisfactory results in the lives of its adherents, due partly to personal misapprehensions, the operative inwardness of true mysticism. It is now time to emphasize the social Gospel, with its attempt to bring Heaven down to Earth, to better the conditions among those with whom we live, to lift up the poor, educate the illiterate, establish dispensaries, clinics and hospitals for the sick, and to do all this in the Name that is above every name, and in the spirit of humility which He manifested.

The religion of the Evangelical must be more than loyalty to an inherited creed, or the assertion of authority by self-appointed leaders. Its very sanctity must compel spiritual acceptance. For the Latin American, as for all thinking people, there is no argu-

ment equal to that of a holy life, of holiness in word
and deed.   And what South America needs is not a
perpetual declaration against the errors and decadence
of Rome, but a deeper earnestness, a more pervasive
odour of sanctity among the Evangelicals themselves.
In any case the life of the missionary will count for
more than his message.   His words will soon be
forgotten ; his manner of life will live on after he is
gone.   The Christian home where pure love holds
sway is a mighty agency for good, especially in a land
where the double standard for the sexes is looked on
as natural and right, and a man is not supposed to
maintain in himself the purity he demands from his
wife.   He will find that the highest culture will be
demanded, and an uncultured worker will here have
less results probably than on any other mission field.
The educated Latin American of the upper classes
represents the highest culture, and only those who
share this gift with him to a very considerable degree
can hope to influence his life.   In one of the Reports
of the Panama Congress of 1916 we read :

" While emphasizing our belief that the work of
a missionary demands special devotion, special gifts
and special temperament, it is our abiding conviction
that, because Latin peoples possess an historic background and atmosphere, gentle and refined manners,
and are uniquely susceptible to culture and the graces
culture brings, the work in Latin America demands
as missionaries men of broad vision, wide culture and
diplomatic temperament.   The Latin is quick to
discern the real lack in his rougher mannered brother
from the aggressive North or elsewhere, and quicker
to resent the implied suggestion that anything or
anybody is good enough for him.   On the other hand,
none is quicker than he to appreciate the effort of
sympathetic students of Latin American customs
and manners.   A Pauline gift of sympathy as well
as a Pauline temper of adaptability seems almost a
perquisite to success in Latin America."

V.

The Slow Progress of Protestant Christianity

1. *The Total Membership in the Three Countries.*

As will be inferred from the above, the progress of Protestantism in this area in the last hundred years has been slow. It is true that only in the last quarter of a century have the Evangelical Missions been manned with a force that was at all adequate to the work to be done. The work before that time was of a pioneering nature, and could not have been expected to give great numerical results. Nevertheless, it must be admitted that the returns have been much less than those which might have resulted from an equal investment of lives and funds in other and less difficult mission fields, and it is well to enquire into the reasons.

A reference to Appendix D (p. 133) will show that, discounting the racial groups such as Anglican, Welsh, Dutch, Scottish, Swedish, etc., whose work is largely or altogether among their own people, with no outside missionary activities, and making generous allowance for the possible membership of a few small groups and independent workers whose statistics could not be secured, the total membership of the Evangelical Churches in the three Republics does not exceed twenty thousand.

2. *Reasons ascribed by Nationals and Others.*

Here again it will be well to allow others to speak on this point, care having been taken to secure the opinion of those whose judgment may be trusted, who are interested in the progress of this work, and are free from sectarian bias.

(*a*) An Argentine Lawyer.

The first to be quoted is an Argentine, a lawyer and educator. He frankly gives the following as the reasons, in his estimation, why the Evangelical Churches have not made greater numerical progress :

" (*a*) Lack of education in the pastorate. The Churches laid themselves out to open evangelical centres in all the country, before a sufficient staff had been developed to direct them. To this must be attributed the stand-off attitude of thousands of men and women who, as children, went to Sunday schools. When such entered national schools and colleges, that is to say when they came up against great philosophical and sociological problems, they soon found that their mental position could not be reconciled with the teaching of the pastors, and that these latter could not satisfy their new vision. They parted company. Hence the present congregations, which constitute the Evangelical Churches, are in a great majority uneducated and lacking in social importance.

" (*b*) Lack of appreciation for the national evangelist. Not infrequently the national evangelist has been treated as an inferior by his foreign colleague. The latter has not always been able to throw off the prejudices of racial, national, and cultural superiority. He has dubbed the native pastor ' brother ' ; but not infrequently, as the vulgar phrase has it, ' whilst staring over his shoulder.' The foreign evangelist has reserved the best posts for himself ; has generally stationed himself nearest the centres of greatest resources, where life is pleasanter and less exposed to privations ; he has, generally speaking, enjoyed fair salaries, while the native ' brother ' has little less than begged his bread, and resigned himself to leaving his children practically unschooled.

" (*c*) Lack of wisdom in the distribution of the Bible. The great distribution of the Bible which now goes forward in this country responds to no true wish to possess it that is felt by the masses. In a very considerable degree this wide distribution is attributable to the following reasons :

1. Groups of colporteurs are engaged in offering it, day by day, and house by house, an advantage possessed by no other book.
2. It is sold at a very low price.
3. It satisfies motives of curiosity.
4. Many people think that in buying the book they are aiding men and institutions which are working sincerely for social welfare. Consequently, rather than figures concerning books sold, statistics of the work really achieved in favour of public morality and attributable to the Bible are to be desired.

" I recall an instance of how misleading it is to formulate conjectures concerning the influence of the Bible based on the number of copies sold, or on the classification of the people who have bought them. I was a law student at La Plata. One day a Bible colporteur presented himself at the University, offering books for next to nothing to the students who hastened to purchase them. In no single instance was there an eagerness to retain possession of a copy ; everyone ridiculed the Book. Some amused themselves with the stories of Genesis ; others sought the Song of Songs ; yet others searched for sexual allusions ; the more moderate sought in the writings of Moses the antecedents of Hebrew law. These were the facts, and they certainly present no basis for satisfaction. I do not think our people are in any condition to understand the Bible, nor to be profoundly moved by it. They lack the necessary preparation. They have not witnessed the marvellous results which the Bible is producing, and has produced, among some other people. For those who do have some understanding, the Bible is a collection of superstitions and utterly opposed to science. There is not even that respect for it which is felt for the Iliad and the Odyssey, in spite of the fact that these poems include all types of myths.

" The day must surely arrive when Bible Societies, who work so unselfishly amongst us and for whom I personally have the most profound respect, will understand : (1) that what should be spread as widely as possible are the Psalms, the Gospels and some of the Epistles, but not the greater proportion of the books of the Old Testament, nor some of the New, such as the Apocalypse. If these books present difficulties to the mind of the believer, we may imagine the effect that is produced on the mind of the non-believer ; and (2) that neither the Bible in general, nor any portion of it, should be put in the hands of the masses without pertinent annotations. Nor should these, except in respect to geographical or historical facts, be given the characteristics of authoritative definitions."

(b) An Argentine Educator.

The writer of the foregoing, as is easily seen, does not favour Protestantism as over against Roman Catholicism, but makes statements devoid of sectarian bias. The same may be said of the next writer to be quoted. He also is a university professor and deeply interested in Christianity, at least intellectually. Replying to a question as to the causes of the slow progress of Evangelical Christianity in these countries, he writes as follows :

" (a) The fact is so because the people of Catholic education—let it not seem to you a paradox—have a conception of religion in general, and of Christianity in particular, more lofty and more respectful than is that of the peoples of Protestant education. But, however we esteem Christianity as a religion of ideals, we lay it up in lavender and live as pagans. Nevertheless, we are horrified with the facility, the Protestant impudence in proclaiming Christ and Christianity at every step, but maintaining a moral level (social, political and private) as low and as little Christian as the Catholic. In respect to collective morality the war proved the great revealer of private morality and daily dealings. Evangelical education does not better habits ; in determined instances it lowers the standard. Hence, away beyond Catholics we are pragmatists. The Epistle of St. James is always *our Epistle*. Hence, we may say—if Protestantism leaves mankind (save for appearances) as pagan as does Catholicism, why change the one for the other ?—the one is as good as the other. Here, in my opinion, is the reason that evangelical work does not make better progress in these countries—*it is devoid of moral efficacy*.

" (*b*) The cause of the backsliding here noticed lies in the circumstance that from Roman Catholic paganism we are heading towards non-religious scepticism, propagated amongst intellectuals through science methods, amongst the masses through social materialism.

" (*c*) The quarrel between the National Government and the Papacy leaves us indifferent : we see in it no religious matter, solely a political difference.

" (*d*) The problem here set out is complex, and much might be written about it. It is true—these people are anxious for good news. But, wearied of Catholicism and disillusioned in respect to Protestantism, we are not disposed to accept other ' good news ' than that of Jesus Christ—none other, not even that of Paul.

" (*e*) I do not believe in the efficacy of the Bible for modern mentality. The war has shown us its failure in the north of Europe and America. The action (especially the morality) of the Evangelical Churches has made its failure very evident in the South."

(*c*) A Foreign Missionary.

A foreign missionary, asked to give his opinion on the point, replied as follows :

" The slow progress of Protestant Christianity in this land is due, I believe, to three fundamental causes :

" 1. *The intellectual atmosphere*. With the intellectual leaders of the country, in university, national colleges, teachers' training schools, and even in primary schools, standing against the Church as organized Christianity, and teaching their agnostic views to the youth of the land, it can be understood why Evangelical Churches find the going hard. It must be very bad for the Roman Catholic Church, in spite of its historical and political predominance. Our Churches are practically forced to work among the lowlier people, who know less about modern intellectual problems and whose lives are so barren that Christianity offers them something worth while. I have noted in my brief contact with the Spanish work what a small percentage of young people remain within the Church as they grow up and come to realize what their intellectual leaders and non-Protestant companions think.

" The remedy lies in an intellectual training for our youth sufficient to make them able to stand upon their own feet ; in an intellectual advance all along the line, for pastors, for Christian young people as teachers in public schools and Sunday schools. There is need also of Protestant national colleges and a Protestant university.

" 2. *Bad administration of mission work.* I must limit my remarks to my own Church, the only one of which I know much :

(a) There have been many insufficiently prepared men admitted into the ministry, and men without promise. The result is a large number of weak Churches, that were begun by some enthusiastic brother, then turned over to preachers unable to make them progress. These weak pastors and weak Churches are the bane of our Mission. They count up in the statistics, however, ' so many churches,' ' so many members '—perfectly dormant though they may be.

(b) Bad administration is seen in many cases where a weak pastor, having ruined one Church is sent to a Church in fair condition, to lay *it* low.

" What is needed is, firstly, a training in the seminaries, with more training of the pastors for *community* and *youth* leadership, and to achieve this, fearlessness on the part of the administrators. Secondly, the appointment of pastors for five years, and if they kill the Churches, they should be discharged from the ministry for incompetence.

" 3. *Lack of spiritual certainty or religious certainty on the part of the Ministry.* Most ministers are greatly confused in regard to religious beliefs, and on the application of Christ's teachings to life. Not knowing how to decide these questions for themselves, they lack prophetic power in their utterances, while, just as fatal and perhaps more evident, they have no definite social message or leadership.

" I believe the minister must courageously bore down to bedrock principles, believe them himself, and ably teach them to his people. He must lead his people into Christ-like activities that, in the face of humanity's need, their souls may not atrophy. In this way society may be best served and come to believe in Christ and in His programme. Finally, the pastor must *believe* that something will happen when he prays, speaks and works."

(*d*) A National Pastor.

The last to be quoted is a national pastor of one of the leading Evangelical Churches. He writes :

" The reasons which have impeded evangelical work from greater progress in the River Plate Republics are doubtless various.

" In my opinion, the inadequacy of our meeting houses and evangelical chapels constitutes an obstacle by no means insignificant. In these countries the Roman Church has great buildings dedicated to worship, and those who are accustomed to frequent these imposing edifices, well furnished and decorated, are repelled by our humble buildings, which frequently do not bear the slightest suggestion of dedication to Christian worship. Further, because the common title of ' Christian ' is given to Roman Catholic and

Evangelical alike, and occasions have not been lacking in which Evangelical ' Missioners ' have spoken of the Roman clergy as Christians and brethren, hence the people say, and with much reason : ' What does it profit us to leave the Church to which we belong and to unite with another Church, if so be we find only that which we have had in the other ? '

" Another reason, in my opinion, lies in the fact that because the evangelical work has so far been directed by foreign missionaries, the great majority of whom are English or North American, the Roman clergy continually use this fact to magnify the exotic character of Protestantism as something exclusively Anglo-Saxon, inadequate and undesirable for Spanish Americans. Not only is it common to hear missionaries referred to as agents of the political ambitions of their home countries in the exploitation and even absorption of Latin America, but also by no means infrequently as explorers with a special mission to prepare the way for the merchant and the man-of-war. I believe that were it possible to prepare the people of these countries themselves to take over the conduct of the work, the progress would be more rapid.

" The lack of adaptation on the part of many missionaries is a serious evil. They are well-educated men, of much consecration to their work, and of great zeal, but they come from countries and surroundings entirely different from those in which they are to work, knowing nothing of the idiosyncracies of the people, lacking even a sufficient mastery of the language, and remain quite outside the life of the people.

" The material advancement of these countries is a source of difficulty. The public is very exacting, the Christian workers need preparation, for without it people think that to listen to them amounts to a waste of time. The trade guilds are systematically opposed to all religion ; hence evangelical workpeople find themselves between two fires. On the one hand are the Pharisees who affirm that there is one sole Church, the Roman, and one sole means of salvation,

membership in her fold, and treat Evangelicals as
heretics, free-masons and atheists ; on the other are
the Sadducees who affirm that there is no resurrection
or other life, and treat us as fanatics and obscurantists,
allies of the bourgeoisie for the better exploitation of
the workers.

" The fact that in the city of Buenos Aires the
Church does not intervene in even fifty per cent. of the
marriages is attributable, in my opinion, to the war
without quarter which the working classes are waging
on such ceremonies, and to the absolute lack of religious instruction amongst the masses of the people.
Men and women alike are unaware of the most elemen-
tary principles even of the Catholic Faith. They
know neither Commandments nor the Apostles' Creed.
The absolute ignorance of religious principles is fright-
ful ; incredible. Hence there is no interest in the
participation of a representative of religion unless it
be in the satisfaction of a vain desire for social pro-
minence. Since the priest charges a fee for the blessing
pronounced over the wedded pair, they just do without
this, save in the case of those desiring a show, which
is within the reach only of the relatively wealthy,
or when there is a feeling of faith, which unfortunately
exists only too rarely.

" I believe that, in spite of the fact that the task
of selling Bibles is relatively easy, the benefit arising
therefrom is insignificant. There are few people who
have the constancy necessary to read the Bible, and of
those who read but few understand anything. On a
certain occasion I was exalting the Bible as the Book
of books before a group of people : within quite a
short period they returned, offering me half a dozen
Bibles at fifty cents apiece (fifteen cents American
money, say sevenpence) as their owners were not
further interested in the reading. In the city of San
Luis a colporteur told me he had journeyed from
door to door during several days, having sold only
eight copies ; but he had been able to realize that
quite seventy-five per cent. of the homes owned a
copy of the Scriptures. Nevertheless, that city lives

in the densest spiritual ignorance, and is absolutely unaware of the glorious message to man which the Bible contains. Many people buy the Bible, quite unaware of the type of message it presents, and not a few in the belief that it is a devotional book recommended by the Roman Church, only to find later that their confessor prohibits its reading.

" I do not think that much real progress will be achieved in these countries until the Gospel is proclaimed by our own people, whose life shall bear witness to the reality of their Christian profession."

3. *The Effect of Evangelical Missions on the Public Consciousness.*

In view of the religious situation, as revealed by these writers, it is only natural and legitimate to ask : What will be the result of the impact of the Protestant message on the consciousness of the people ? If in the last century the Protestant Churches in this region have not made that numerical advance which many of their supporters had hoped to see, is the value of this work to be depreciated or judged only by the number of its members and adherents ? Or may there be a higher value or other values which one may seek ?

(*a*) Reflex influence on the dominant Church.

The writer believes that the influence of Protestantism on the Roman Catholic Church is one of its most important contributions to the advancement of religious truth in Latin America.

The Roman Catholic Church has been roused from its self-complacency and lethargy to a greater degree of internal reform with beneficial results. Priests can no longer mumble a Mass in an unknown tongue, with complete omission of a sermon or other religious teaching in the vernacular. Sermons, and good sermons, are now being preached, and it detracts but little from them if the orator concludes with an attack on Protestantism and a warning to his people to beware of its influence. The priesthood has been compelled to better its own moral standing. Better schools, both of State and Church, have been established because of the introduction of new and modern methods, and to prevent a wholesale registering of children and young people in the Protestant institutions. Roman Catholic universities have been founded to provide the same courses as the State institutions, and yet keep the youth under the influence of the Church. Homes for working men have been built, hospitals and clinics for the poor opened, the Bible or portions thereof circulated by Church authorization, and reading in the vernacular in the public services made obligatory.

In centres where the Young Men's Christian Association has established its social programme, the Church has felt compelled to adopt the same or similar methods. Catholic Associations have been formed, and summer camps conducted along the lines laid down by the Association. Athletics have been encouraged, better morals for youth advocated, better literature circulated, and all this has been done while openly and rabidly attacking the institution whose methods were being copied.

(b) Good in Protestantism acknowledged by some Roman Catholic leaders.

Some of the leaders of the Roman Catholic hierarchy are willing to admit that they do well in imitating the Protestants and following their methods, as shown by the reported statement of a Bishop of that Church, made during an important gathering of Roman Catholic forces in a neighbouring Republic. The question of the rapid extension of Protestantism was under discussion, and some of the leaders proposed harsh measures in order to suppress it. The Bishop, replying, is said to have declared that, in at least three things, they might well imitate the Evangelicals. " They have a ministry which is respected and worthy of respect, while our clergy are the laughing-stock of the country. They practise temperance, which we ought to do. They put the Bible in circulation, which we also ought to be doing." It is reported that, as a result of that Conference, a cheap edition of the New Testament has been printed and widely circulated, and the Archbishop has also decreed that all parish priests, under seventy years of age, must, in every service they conduct, read some portion of Holy Scripture in the vernacular.

But Evangelical Missions are justified, not alone by their reflex influence on the leaders of the Roman Catholic community, but especially by the results shown in changed lives and character among their converts. So marked is this result that advertisements for help sometimes add " Protestant preferred," thus rendering tribute to the greater honesty and faithfulness of the worker belonging to the evangelical community. Drunkards and outcasts have been redeemed and placed in positions of usefulness, homes have been re-established, purity of life exalted, and religion elevated to its proper place in the conscience of the community.

(c) The future of the dominant Church.

As to the future of Roman Catholicism in these lands, no one can make a definite statement. Some people still hold that there is a possibility of reform from within, which would give the Church spiritual power and influence in the community. History does not encourage this belief. Others hope to see it continue to decay, and finally to disappear from the scene. This is also unlikely, and, moreover, is not to be desired. It contains too much that is good and its history is too redolent of the sweetness of lives given to its service in utter abandonment of self to allow one to entertain, with any degree of pleasure, the thought of such a termination of its activities.

It seems more probable that it will continue its existence as an increasingly social power, adapting itself in external appearances to changing conditions,

G

urged on by a Protestant minority in the population, and will contribute to the solution of many of the social and spiritual problems of the times.

There are those who believe that, due to the influence of the Christian associations and other inter-confessional groups, a third organization will emerge from among those who reject the traditional Roman Catholicism, believing it to be a spent force, and who are unwilling to accept Protestantism because of its emphasis on theology. This, however, is still a question, and there are but few who look on the present situation as likely to produce such a phenomenon in the near future.

VI.

Unevangelized Groups and Regions

ONE of the seeming errors in the strategy of the Evangelical Missions in the past has been the tendency, if not the definite policy, to establish and develop work in the large centres and to leave the country districts unoccupied. It is true that the bulk of the population is in the cities, as is so often the case in undeveloped and under-populated countries. In this sense Buenos Aires is Argentina, and Montevideo is Uruguay, and Asunción is Paraguay. While this is true, the fact remains that a study of the map shows that there are hundreds of thousands of people in the country regions of these three Republics who are altogether untouched by the evangelical message, or who have at the best but a meagre understanding of even its most essential truths.

This concentration in the large cities, at the time when Evangelical Missions first entered the country a century ago, can easily be explained. The country was then but sparsely settled by Europeans or their descendants, large areas were still in the possession of wild and savage Indian tribes, revolutions were frequent and human life was cheap. Even in Buenos Aires, on such occasions, when under military dictators, bare existence was most precarious and, as we have seen, at least two attempts to establish evangelical work in that city failed. But the most important missionary boards, having begun in this way, have found it difficult to change, and some have never extended their work beyond the city boundaries. Some Missions have gradually entered other large centres, but there is a vast territory remaining unoccupied. Some of the more recent arrivals have reversed the usual order and have begun their work in the smaller towns, along the different railway lines. Among such are the Christian Brethren in Rio Cuarto, in the Province of Córdoba ; the Mennonites in the Province of Buenos Aires ; the Apostolic Church in Tucumán and one of the neighbouring villages, in the Province of the same name ; and the Christian and Missionary Alliance in the southern part of the Province of Buenos Aires. The Evangelical Union of South America has also limited its work to the smaller towns in the same Province, and the work of the Inland South America Missionary Union is primarily for the Indians of Brazil and Paraguay, with centres in the smaller towns of Paraguay, and headquarters in Posadas, in the Territory of Misiones, in Argentina.

In Uruguay, the capital city is occupied by the Methodists, the Southern Baptists, the Salvation Army and the Free Brethren. The first three have also entered some of the smaller towns. In Montevideo, too, are the two Christian associations and the Anglican Church, while the Scots Church of Buenos Aires sends its minister to take an occasional service for the members of the colony ; but the people of Spanish speech in the country districts are almost completely deprived of contact with Protestantism.

In Paraguay, an immense land with but few roads and but one short railway, the situation is worse. The Disciples of Christ, the only American Board working in the country, have not yet extended their work outside Asunción. The Free Brethren use this city as a centre, but are also doing a unique work along the river by means of a motor launch. The Salvation Army is confining itself to Asunción, and the Inland South America Missionary Union has a small work in one or two towns along the railway and in Villa Encarnación, on the river, on the very frontier of the country. The whole of the Republic otherwise is unoccupied, save for the work of the South American Missionary Society among the Indians of the Chaco ; an independent worker who is a qualified physician at Belén, near the river port of Concepción, and the newly founded colony of Mennonites in a region hitherto unoccupied by members of the white race.

Mention has been made in another section of the remarkable success of the Waldensian colonists in Uruguay. Other nationalities have established smaller groups in other sections of the region, but they have had but an ephemeral existence and have disappeared, or have been absorbed and engulfed by the surrounding Latin population.

In recent years, the Bible Societies have endeavoured to reach the country districts and smaller towns by means of specially made automobiles, and have had good success in disposing of their publications. The present secretary of the American Society in Buenos Aires makes frequent visits into the interior, and has a special coach for visiting the Waldensian colonists in Uruguay and other scattered groups in that country. The Brethren, whose centre is in Córdoba, have a coach for use in and around that city, and the Evangelical Union of South America employs the same method in the Province of Buenos Aires. But the great majority of the people, of many distinct nationalities and a varied religious background, who live in the sparsely settled districts of the three Republics are without any living contact with evangelical forces. Such religious instruction as they may obtain is limited to the very occasional visits of an itinerant priest, or a mission conducted by a group of priests. There is a very large number of people who are completely beyond the reach of even these missionaries.

The lack of communication in the country districts, except along the railways, makes itineration difficult, even in summer, and practically impossible during the rainy season of winter. Good asphalt or concrete roads, so familiar to the residents of the United Kingdom and of the United States, save in the immediate vicinity of the cities, are generally lacking. Country roads are made impossible by the frequent and heavy rains. Motor-cars are coming into more general use,

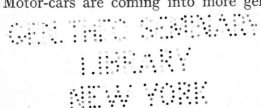

especially the omnipresent Ford, and country roads are being improved. But there are vast regions into which these cars have never penetrated, where the usual travel and transport is by bullock cart, and even this becomes impossible at certain seasons.

In the cities, of course, there are well-paved streets, and avenues and boulevards as smooth and well-kept as are those of London, Paris or New York, and there is every kind of communication between these centres, by rail, by water and by air, but it will be many years before any of these advantages will be found in the hinterland. In these unevangelized regions there are also many thousands of people of evangelical antecedents, who need the ministrations of the Church. This fact is being recognized by some of the home organizations and help is being offered.

The Scots Presbyterian Church, for example, has recently made an effort to care for scattered ranchmen and other colonists in Patagonia. A few years ago a survey of the region was made by the Rev. Douglas W. Bruce, now minister of the St. Andrew's Scots Presbyterian Church, Buenos Aires, and, on his recommendation, a minister was sent out to undertake this work. But he soon returned home and the thousands of Scotsmen who live in that sparsely populated region, which reaches down to the Straits of Magellan and includes the great sheep-raising districts of Argentina and Chile, are again without spiritual ministrations. This is a work that should appeal to Presbyterians in the homeland, who could well afford to sustain a permanent mission in this far-off corner of the world where so many of their own faith and kin are living under conditions that severely test both their physique and their spiritual life.

Not only in the sparsely settled regions are there people without adequate spiritual help, but there are also industrial groups in or near the large centres which are completely neglected. The workshops of the railways bring together thousands of men, with their families, and form homogeneous groups which, if they are to be interested, demand a special presen-

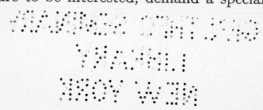

tation of the claims of religion. So far as the writer knows, there has been no effort made to meet this need, which is primarily for English-speaking workmen, save the work of the Anglicans in Rosario and Junín, Argentina, and Sapucay, Paraguay.

The immense packing-houses scattered along the littoral, such as those of Liebig, Swift, Armour and others, in Argentina, Paraguay and Uruguay, form populous centres in which much work could be done, not only in the way of evangelism, but also in providing schools for the children and, particularly, in providing for the very poor and those who are out of employment through the frequent shutting down of the industry or the reducing of the number of employees. The majority of the workmen, especially in the tasks that require great physical strength and are at the same time the least attractive because of the nature of the work, are foreigners, such as Poles, Russians, Czecho-slovaks, etc., and, when left without work, their position becomes pitiable in the extreme. They cannot speak the language of the country with any facility and cannot readily find other work, and thus they soon become objects of charity.

The Methodist Episcopal Mission has for years carried on a very useful work in Montevideo, in what is known as " The Hill District," which reaches many of the families whose bread-winners find employment in the great packing-houses nearby. Church services are maintained and a considerable congregation has been built up. But of even more importance is the work among the young people, through well-staffed day schools, Sunday schools, and recreation centres. The help given to the needy has been freed, as far as possible, from the taint of charity, in that work has been pro-vided, when practicable, and shops have been main-tained in which all kinds of cast-off articles donated by the public have been cleaned, remodelled, and sold to the poor at a mere fraction of their original value. In this way self-respect has been inculcated and the general public has had its sympathy awakened

to the need in its midst. Gifts of money have also
been substantial and this " Pan-American Institute "
stands as an example of the kind of uplift work which
might be done in other similar communities.

Open-air preaching has been carried on at intervals
by different groups, but does not seem to have produced
any special results. The Salvation Army, of course,
uses this method, and the Free Brethren also conduct
tent missions in the cities. The Federation of Young
People of the Methodist Episcopal Church carried
out a series of meetings in the principal square of
Montevideo a year or so ago, and reported good attention on the part of the public.   Such meetings are
generally limited to the singing of hymns, to attract
the passer-by, and an address. When the speaker is
a national, if he has the gift of expressing himself
well, with the fervour and enthusiasm characteristic
of his race, he is likely to be heard with respect and
will probably be applauded. If he is a foreigner,
Latin courtesy may prevent any untoward demon-
stration of disapproval, especially if he speaks the
language well, but his message will not have the same
effect in convincing his hearers. In these recent times,
particularly, it would be difficult for a foreigner,
especially an Anglo-Saxon, to carry on this work with
any degree of success in either Argentina or Uruguay.
In Paraguay there is less nationalistic sentiment, and,
hence, less feeling against the foreigner.

The coast-line of Argentina and Uruguay is notice-
ably free from islands.   A few very small ones, near
Montevideo and Buenos Aires, are used for the erection
of light-houses or as quarantine stations, and no
religious work is attempted in any of these islands.
Nor is it likely that such work would be permitted
by the Governments concerned. The only important
group, both as to size and population, is that of the
Falkland Islands, off Argentina. These lie to the far
south, between fifty and fifty-five degrees south
latitude, and belong to Great Britain. Readers of
these lines will recall that it was in the vicinity of

these islands that one of the great naval battles of the recent War was fought. There are only about two thousand inhabitants, half of whom live in Port Stanley, the capital. Almost all are British, and all are English-speaking. The religious work is entirely in the care of the Anglican Church and there is a cathedral, which was completed at the beginning of the present century at a cost of over £10,000. The industry of the islands is sheep-farming, and many of the farmers are Scots, from the highlands, and of Gaelic speech. Outside Port Stanley religious work is maintained by visits from the clergy, and education is carried on by means of itinerant schoolmasters, who visit the widely-scattered cottages and remain in the vicinity of each for some weeks.

Keppell Island, near West Falkland, is of historic interest to students of Missions, since it was intimately connected with the beginnings of the work of the South American Missionary Society. After the disasters which have already been referred to, the Society leased this island from the Government, and used it as a centre for the training of native Fuegian boys. It was here that Bishop Stirling, then in priest's orders, landed on January 30th, 1863, and began his great work in South America. It was here also that Mr. W. B. Grubb, famous in the work of the South American Missionary Society in the Chaco, had his first experience with the Indians.

There are a few other islands belonging to Argentina at the southernmost extremity of the Continent, among them the eastern part of the island of Tierra del Fuego. The penal settlement of the Republic, Ushuaia, which in some degrees corresponds to the " Isle du Diable " of the coast of the Guianas belonging to France, is located on one of them, and there are a few Indians along the Beagle Channel. Apart from these, there are no inhabitants, and the islands are of little importance to the country. The Indians on these islands and the neighbouring mainland, now fewer in number, are in the same degraded condition in which they were found by Allen Gardiner, the great naturalist Charles Darwin, and others who came after them, and it seems likely that they are destined to disappear in a short time.

The various Missions that work in these Republics, as in all Latin America, have vied with each other in following a set programme, from which they could with difficulty depart. It is quite possible that by so doing they have clouded the real issue, and have unconsciously entered into competition with each other, while the main task of reaching the most needy classes has been left largely untouched.

Certain it is that any new Mission coming into the field should seek the unoccupied spaces, or the groups that to-day are neglected. An itinerant Mission, going here and there, as weather and other conditions permit, with but little thought of building up a church constituency, could be of immense help to the outlying districts and to the groups that for commercial reasons are segregated from the mass of citizens.

There are also certain other groups for whom nothing is being done. Chief among these, in their pathetic need, are the lepers. The disease is said to be rapidly increasing, yet but little is being done to prevent its spreading. Leper asylums (leprosaria) are maintained, one in each of the three capitals, but, taken together, they do not care for more than three hundred patients. The accommodation in Montevideo and Asunción is of the simplest and crudest, and in Buenos Aires the lepers, men, women and children, with a separation of the sexes, are segregated in one of the pest hospitals.

One of the Churches in Buenos Aires has taken some interest in these unfortunates, providing, especially at Christmas time, certain dainties, and sending a word of cheer. The American Mission to Lepers of recent years has helped in a similar way, and, through its representative in South America, has also endeavoured to arouse a greater interest in the disease and its treatment on the part of the medical faculties and the Governments. Plans for better buildings are now being considered, and an awakened interest is being taken in prophylactic measures, but in respect of spiritual work nothing is being done. It is unlikely that opposition would be offered by the hospitals or Government authorities against such spiritual work, but, in all probability, the dominant Church, which now does nothing, would interfere and try to prevent any Protestant effort being made.

There are many Moslems, Buddhists and representatives of other Eastern cults among the population, but so scattered that it would be difficult to segregate them as objects of special religious interest. The Armenian pastor in Buenos Aires, whose work has already been mentioned, not only maintains regular services for his people, with evident good results, but he also meets and offers his services to new immigrants of his own nationality, especially young women who are coming out to relatives or to find occupations, regardless of their religious affiliations.

Possibly only in this way, through converted members of their own race, can non-European groups be reached. To bring such workers to this country would seem to be difficult, yet it is not impossible, as is shown by the remarkable work in Brazil among the Japanese by one of their own number who came from Japan for that purpose.

Immigrants from Protestant countries of Europe are, in general, looked after in the larger cities by their own communities, and in Buenos Aires and Montevideo these communities of German, Norwegian, Swedish and Danish, have their own pastor. But in the smaller towns and country districts they are generally without religious care, and are destined, within one or two generations, to be absorbed by the dominant Church, or become entirely non-religious. All British and American Protestants, especially those that live in the large cities, can find church life in the Anglican, the Scots Presbyterian or the Methodist Episcopal Churches, each of which maintains an extensive work both inside and outside the large cities.

The Salvation Army carries on its usual activities on behalf of the poor and new arrivals. Through its Homes it cares especially for sailors. There are also Missions to Seamen, including a well-managed institution in Buenos Aires, under the direction of the Anglican Church.

The Young Men's Christian Association in Buenos Aires, through a secretary, finds occupation for many immigrants from Germany, Poland, Russia and other countries. The Young Women's Christian Association also conducts an employment bureau, which is of great service to women who find themselves without employment. Women are also met at incoming boats and steamers, and cared for until claimed by relatives or otherwise assured of protection.

To sum up this study of the unoccupied or unevangelized regions within the area under review, and by reference to the map given, it will be seen that there are 780 evangelical workers in Argentina, seventy-five in Uruguay and fifty-seven in Paraguay. This makes a total of 912, not counting wives, or a grand total roughly speaking of 1,520.

The Province of Buenos Aires, the " Queen Province " of the nation and the centre of its activities, with about one-seventh of the total population of the three Republics, has 340 workers, excluding wives.

In Uruguay, there is one worker, not counting wives, to every twenty thousand of the population, one to every fifteen thousand in Paraguay, and in Argentina one to just a little over every thirteen thousand of the population.

In eight provinces or territories of Argentina, among a population of over a quarter of a million, there is not reported a single evangelical worker.

In the provinces and territories of Argentina, as in Paraguay and Uruguay, where there are workers reported, these are not to be found in the rural districts, but almost invariably in the larger towns and cities.

Those reported for the Province of Buenos Aires, for example, are very largely grouped in the city of the same name, and those in Córdoba are almost exclusively in that city. This means that almost the total rural population is left unevangelized, although workers may be reported as occupying this or that political division.

VII.

The Indians

WORK among the Indians is limited to three organizations, the chief of which is the South American Missionary Society, which works in the Chaco region of Argentina and Paraguay. There is a small independent Mission, with its centre in San Pedro, in the Province of Jujuy, for which statistics are not available. The Inland South America Missionary Union has a centre in Posadas, Argentina, but its work is almost entirely in Paraguay and Brazil. In addition to these, Dr. Lindsay carries on an independent work in Belén, Paraguay, and has prepared a complete translation of the New Testament in Guarain, which was published by the British and Foreign Bible Society in 1913.

For the few remaining members of the tribes which once attracted the active sympathy of Captain Gardiner, in the southern end of the continent, nothing is being done, and it can be but a question of time until they vanish from the scene. The encroachments of the white man's industries on their original domain are each year greater, and before them the aboriginal inhabitants must perforce disappear.

In regard to the work of the South American Missionary Society, in Paraguay and Argentina, one of its veteran missionaries has kindly contributed the following paragraphs :

" *The Gran Chaco.*

" The geographical name of the *Gran Chaco* is a very elastic term and very loosely used, but in a general way it is the name given to an extensive tract of country, situated in the heart of the

Continent, and stretching from twenty to twenty-nine degrees south latitude, having as its eastern boundary the River Paraguay, while westward, it extends to the foothills of the Andes. Two great rivers, the Bermejo and Pilcomayo, and several smaller but considerable streams, flow through it to join the waters of the Paraguay.

" Its central parts remain, even to-day, wild and inhospitable, occupied by nomadic tribes of Indians, known and unknown, who live by fishing in the swamps and streams, by hunting the deer and ostrich and other game found in the grassy plains and dense forests, and by the cultivation of a few common vegetables. But the circle of barbarism is growing narrower day by day. From all sides civilization creeps steadily forward. Small towns are springing up on the fringes, roads and railways are penetrating the interior, timber establishments are being set up at suitable places, while cattle farms and modest attempts at agriculture are being made along the rivers and in the well-watered lands of more remote regions. Gradually the rude huts and little clearings of the savages are being replaced by permanent houses and extensive plantations of the more cultured settlers. The missionaries of the South American Missionary Society have contributed no small part in this matter, though their aims were not the exploration and opening up of the country to civilization, but rather the social welfare and spiritual concern of the aborigines.

" The Paraguayan Chaco Mission.

" The missionary work of our Church to the aborigines of the Gran Chaco took practical shape in the year 1890, when Mr. W. Barbrooke Grubb boldly set out to investigate the unexplored territory of the Paraguayan Chaco and to evangelize its unknown inhabitants. Journeys to the interior and wanderings among the people led to the formation of little mission stations, which were abandoned as more suitable sites were found, until eventually in 1895 land was

purchased and building commenced at a place called
Waikthlatingmangyalwa, nearly a hundred miles from
the River Paraguay. This became the central station,
from which journeys were made in every direction,
and to which were attracted numbers of the Lengua
and of the neighbouring tribes.

" Great success attended every branch of the
work among these simple folk untainted with the vices
of civilization. Children were gathered together and
instructed. Young men were trained in all branches
of industry suitable to their life and circumstances,
such as building, fencing, carpentry, and cattle work.
Young women were drilled in all kinds of domestic
duties and several trained as teachers and nurses.
The social life of the people was not forgotten. All
that was good in their old customs was retained, and
new and wholesome features were introduced to
brighten and improve the outlook of the community.
Evils of infanticide, drunkenness and witchcraft
diminished as the Gospel gradually won its way into
their hearts. Eventually a strong Church was formed
in their midst, and a number of young men were
trained as evangelists to teach their own people living
in the surrounding villages. The central station was
ultimately removed to Makthlaway, the present
thriving Christian colony with its church and school,
farm and workshop, shop and village.

" Westward towards the River Pilcomayo there
are two tribes of Indians called by the Lengua ' Suhin '
and ' Towothli,' which were known to the old chroni-
clers as ' Chunupi ' and ' Enimaga ' respectively. As
far back as 1896 efforts were made to reach and subdue
to the Gospel these two warlike tribes. For seven years
the work continued with a moderate amount of success,
during which time a convenient site was acquired
and considerable knowledge obtained of the customs,
language and distribution of the people. Owing to
physical changes, chiefly a prolonged drought, the
Indians migrated to another district and the Mission
was temporarily abandoned. After a lapse of several
years the Mission was reopened at a more suitable

place, but the lack of workers combined with the
character of the people militated against real success,
and it is only during the past five years that definite
progress has been made. This station of Nanawa has
now its church and school and other mission buildings,
and its regular services, and the first candidates have
been accepted for baptism. It must be admitted,
however, that it still remains a hard field to work,
much patience is required and the response is poor,
and the political troubles arising out of the frontier
disputes of Paraguay and Bolivia hamper the movements of the missionaries, and introduce an atmosphere
inimical to the growth of spirituality among the natives.

" *The Argentine Chaco Mission.*

" Emboldened by the success of the work among
the Lengua, it was decided to extend the Mission
to other tribes lying to the north and west in Bolivia
and Argentina, and for that purpose it would be
necessary to establish stations on the western side
of the Gran Chaco. Accordingly, in 1911, experienced
missionaries were selected and sent to Northern
Argentina to study prevailing conditions, in order to
complete a line of stations across the whole region
from the banks of the Paraguay to the foothills of the
Andes. During the next three years itinerant journeys
were undertaken and probable sites for stations were
selected. The various tribes were visited and identified,
their distribution noted and a working knowledge of
the languages acquired. Friendly relations having
been established, reports were sent home, together
with an appeal for sixteen workers, but the War
prevented the realization of any well-considered plan
for linking up all these Mission posts by the occupation
of strategic points, suitable for evangelizing the
various peoples, yet sufficiently connected with each
other for mutual help in time of need. All that could
be done under the circumstances was to hold the
western position ; and to try to keep in touch with
the peoples already influenced. Land was secured,

H

and, at the close of the fateful year 1914, the Mataco Mission was started on the eastern bank of the Rio Bermejo.

" The work thus begun developed along the usual lines, educational, industrial, medical and evangelistic. Progress was normal, the simple folk were attracted to the station, interest was kindled by short addresses on the great truths of God's Word, and after seven years' work the first converts came forward and were baptized by Bishop Every on April 3rd, 1922. The five years that followed have been years of remarkable development both in numbers and spiritual growth. Owing to the ravages of the river, which threatened the Mission with destruction, the present station is the third one built, the other two having been abandoned without loss of life or property. Now it is fully equipped with church and school, dispensary and office, store and workshop, the native adherents suitably provided with gardens and dwelling places, and, in spite of the natural poverty of the people, everything breathes an atmosphere of contentment and joyousness. Baptism has been followed by confirmation and the fuller flow of church life. Already the Baptismal Roll numbers eighty-six, and of these forty-two are confirmed and regular communicants."

The Inland South America Missionary Union.

The Rev. John Hay states that the great majority of the population of Paraguay proper consist of pure and mixed *Guarani* Indians.

Various attempts at work among these Indians have been made, but with little result. The Methodist Episcopal Church carried on work for a long period, but finally, about 1914, gave it up. The South American Missionary Society attempted day-school work in Villa Rica, but relinquished it after several years (1903).

Paraguay is recognized as a very difficult field owing to the fanaticism and illiteracy of its people and the fact that, while Spanish is the official language, Guarani is the language commonly spoken.

The Inland South America Missionary Union, a society with headquarters in Scotland, began work in the north of Paraguay in 1902, and outside Asunción, the capital, and the *Chaco* Indian area, it is the only Mission in the country. The greatest development has taken place in the south, where work was began in 1908.

The people are nominally Roman Catholics, but in spirit still pagan. Many would say that morally they have reached a lower level than before the Jesuits brought about their nominal conversion.

Among such a people progress has been slow. Converts have been subjected to much persecution and the missionaries themselves have often been in danger. During the last few years, however, there have been evidences of much greater response to the Gospel message, especially in south Paraguay, where there is the greatest density of population.

This Mission has been making considerable progress recently, and has now four foreign and two indigenous workers in the north, while in the south there are eleven foreign and seven indigenous workers at eight stations and out-stations.

Although it was not the original purpose of this Mission to enter Argentina, work has been organized in five centres, including Posadas, under seven foreign and eight indigenous workers.

This was necessitated by the fact that Christians from Paraguay and Posadas were so successful in winning converts that the problem of their care had to be faced. No other Missions were at work in these districts, and there is the hope that a vigorous and rapidly growing Church will be developed.

Many Spaniards, Italians and Germans are entering Paraguay at the present time and the problem of its evangelization cannot be confined to the purely Indian population. The work in such areas tends to embrace all who can be reached of whatever race or colour.

APPENDICES.

APPENDIX A.
ARGENTINA.—SUMMARY AND STATISTICS.*
PARAGUAY.—SUMMARY AND STATISTICS.*
URUGUAY.—SUMMARY AND STATISTICS.*

APPENDIX B.
EVANGELICAL SCHOOLS.

APPENDIX C.
THEOLOGICAL SEMINARIES.
BIBLE INSTITUTES.

APPENDIX D.
THE PRINCIPAL NON-ROMAN CATHOLIC GROUPS.

APPENDIX E.
NOTE ON OCCUPATION.

---

*Most of the areas and populations given in these Statistics are taken from *The Statesman's Year Book.*

APPENDIX A.

ARGENTINA.

SUMMARY.

Area	1,153,119 square miles.
Population	10,348,189.
Density	8.97 per square mile.
Principal Mission Stations	75.
Missions and Societies ..	42.
Foreign Workers	454 (not including wives).
National Workers ..	326 (not including wives).
Protestant Community ..	Probably 100,000, including all Protestant foreigners.

ARGENTINA.

THE PRINCIPAL NON-ROMAN CATHOLIC ORGANIZATIONS.

1. The Anglican Church (A.Ch.).
2. The Apostolic Church (Ap.Ch.).
3. The Armenian Church (Ar.Ch.).
4. The American Bible Society (A.B.S.).
5. The Assemblies of God (A.G.).
6. The British and Foreign Bible Society (B.F.B.S.).
7. Christian Missions in Many Lands (C.M.M.L.).
8. Christian and Missionary Alliance (C.M.A.).
9. Church of the Nazarene (C.N.).
10. The Disciples of Christ, or United Christian Missionary Society (U.C.M.S.).
11. The Danish Church (D.Ch.).
12. The Dutch Reformed Church from Holland (D.R.Ch.H.).
13. The Dutch Reformed Church from South Africa (D.R.Ch.A.).
14. Evangelical Union of South America (E.U.S.A.).
15. The Free Brethren from the U.S.A. (F.B.).
16. The German Evangelical Church (G.Ev.Ch.).
17. Independent Organizations (Ind.).
18. Inland South America Missionary Union (I.S.A.M.U.)
19. The Mennonite Church (M.Ch.).
20. The Methodist Episcopal Church (M.E.F.B.).
21. The Norwegian Church (Nor.Ch.).
22. South American Missionary Society (S.A.M.S.).
23. Southern Baptist Convention (S.B.C.).
24. The Salvation Army (S.A.).
25. The Seventh-Day Adventists (S.D.A.).
26. Swedish Free Mission (S.F.M.).
27. San Pedro Mission to Indians (S.P.I.).
28. The Scots Presbyterian Church (S.P.Ch.).
29. The Pentecostal Church (Pen.Ch.).
30. The United Lutheran Church Mission (U.L.C.).
31. World's Sunday School Association (W.S.S.A.).
32. Women's Christian Temperance Union (W.C.T.U.).
33. The Orthodox Church, Russian (O.Ch.R.).
34. The Orthodox Church, Greek (O.Ch.G.).
35. The Orthodox Church of Antioch, Syrian (O.Ch.S.).
36. Jewish Synagogues (J.S.).
37. The Church of the Latter-Day Saints, Mormon (L.D.S.).
38. The Welsh Church, in Chubut (Wel.Ch.).
39. The Evangelical Christian Church (E.C.Ch.).
40. The Young Men's Christian Association (Y.M.C.A.).
41. The Young Women's Christian Association (Y.W.C.A.).
42. The Committee on Co-operation in Latin America (C.C.L.A.).

ARGENTINA.

District.	Area.	Population.	Density.	Principal Mission Stations.	Missions.	Foreign Workers.*	National Workers.*	Protestant Community.
Federal District Buenos Aires and Martin Garcia Island	72	1,972,823	27400.32	Buenos Aires	A.Ch. Ar.Ch. C.N. U.C.M.S. D.Ch. D.R.Ch.H. U.L.C. G.Ev.Ch. Nor.Ch. S.F.M. C.C.L.A. A.B.S. B.F.B.S. S.P.Ch. Pen.Ch. W.C.T.U. W.S.S.A. O.Ch.R. O.Ch.G. J.S. L.D.S. E.C.Ch. Y.M.C.A. Y.W.C.A. S.D.A. A.G. C.M.M.L. M.E.F.B. S.A. S.B.C. O.Ch.S.			
	72	1,972,823	27400.32	1 Station.	31 Missions	150†	100†	45,000†

* Not including wives.   † Carefully estimated.

ARGENTINA—Continued.

Provinces.	Area.	Population.	Density.	Principal Mission Stations.	Missions.	Foreign Workers.*	National Workers.*	Protestant Community.
Buenos Aires	117,777	2,814,601	23.89	Algarrobal	S.A.M.S.			
				Azul	C.M.A.			
				Alberdi	S.A.M.S.			
				Bahia Blanca	S.A.			
					S.D.A.			
					M.E.F.B.			
					S.A.M.S.			
				Bolivar	A.G.			
				Campana	E.U.S.A.			
				Camerero	S.D.A.			
				Casares	M.Ch.			
				Guaminí	C.M.A.			
				Laprida	C.M.A.			
				Mercedes	M.E.F.B.			
				Mar del Plata	Ind.			
				Olavarria	C.M.A.			
				Piqua	E.U.S.A.			
				Pehuajó	M.Ch.			
				San Nicolás	E.U.S.A.			
				San Fernando	E.U.S.A.			
				Suarez	E.U.S.A.			
				Tandil	E.U.S.A.			
				Trenque Lauquen	M.Ch.			
				Tres Arroyos	E.U.S.A.			
					S.A.M.S.			
					S.A.			
				Quilmes	C.M.M.L.			
				Lanus	C.M.M.L.			
					M.E.F.B.			
				Barracas	S.P.Ch.			
					S.B.C.			
				Temperley	S.P.Ch.			
				Escalada	S.P.Ch.			
				Villa del Parque	U.L.C.			
				Urquiza	S.A.M.S.			
				La Plata	M.E.F.B.			
					S.B.C.			
				Belgrano	S.P.Ch.			
					A.Ch.			
				Florida	S.D.A.			
				Martinez	M.E.F.B.			
				Chivilcoy	M.E.F.B.			
				Chascomus	S.P.Ch.			
				Balcarce	M.E.F.B.			
				Lomas de Zamora	M.E.F.B.			
	117,777	2,814,601	23.89	36 Stations	14 Missions	180	160	50,000

* Not including wives.

Provinces.	Area.	Population.	Density.	Principal Mission Stations.	Missions.	Foreign Workers.*	National Workers.*	Protestant Community.
Santa Fé..	50,713	1,214,571	23.95	Rosario	M.E.F.B. C.M.M.L. S.D.A. S.A.M.S. A.Ch.			
				Santa Fé	C.M.M.L. M.E.F.B.	18	18	
Córdoba ..	66,912	970,971	14.51	Rio Segundo	C.M.M.L.			
				Huinca Renancó	F.B.			
				Belle Ville	C.M.M.L.			
				Alta Gracia	C.M.M.L.			
				Córdoba	M.E.F.B. S.B.C. C.M.M.L.			
				Rio Cuarto	F.B.			
				Villa María	C.M.M.L.			
				La Cumbre	C.M.M.L.	13	8	
Entre Rios	29,241	555,337	18.99	Concordia	I.S.A.M.U. S.A. S.B.C. M.E.F.B.			
				Puiggari	S.D.A.			
				Paraná	S.D.A. M.E.F.B.			
				Urdinarrain	S.B.C.			
				Rosario de Talá	M.E.F.B.			
				Colon	M.E.F.B.	44	15	
Corrientes	33,535	413,648	12.33	Libres	I.S.A.M.U.			
				Mercedes	S.D.A.			
				Corrientes	S.D.A. S.B.C.	7	8	
San Luis..	29,035	149,722	5.16	San Luis	C.M.M.L.			
				San Martin	C.M.M.L.	—	2	
Santiago del Estero	55,385	350,816	6.33	Santiago del Estero	C.M.M.I.	2	—	
Tucumán..	10,422	409,358	39.28	Tucumán	C.M.M.L. Ap.Ch.	4	1	
Mendoza..	56,502	384,090	6.80	Mendoza	M.E.F.B. S.B.C.			
				Junín	M.E.F.B.	2	6	
San Juan..	37,865	156,433	4.13	San Juan	M.E.F.B.	—	2	
La Rioja..	37,839	93,408	2.47	Nil	..			
Catamarca	36,800	120,422	3.27	Catamarca	C.M.M.L.	1	—	
Salta ..	48,302	162,424	3.36	Salta	S.A.M.S.	8	1	
Jujuy ..	14,802	87,993	5.95	San Pedro	S.P.I.	3	—	
	507,353	5,069,193	10.0	29 Stations	11 Missions	102	61	

*The figures in these columns denote the total number of workers (not including wives) in each Province.

ARGENTINA—Continued.

Territories.	Area.	Population.	Density.	Principal Mission Stations.	Missions.	Foreign Workers.*	National Workers.*	Protestant Community.
Misiones ..	11,511			Posadas San Ignacio	I.S.A.M.U. I.S.A.M.U.	11	2	
Formosa ..	41,402			Nil	..	—	—	
Chaco ..	52,741			Nil	..	—	—	
La Pampa	56,320			Santa Rosa de Toay 25 de Mayo General Pico	M.Ch. A.G. C.M.A.	3	3	
Neuquén ..	40,530	491,572	.93	Nil	..	—	—	
Rio Negro	79,805			Nil	..	—	—	
Chubut ..	93,427			Comodoro Rivadavia Rawson 16 de Octubre Bryn Crwn	D.R.Ch.A. S.A.M.S. Wel.Ch. Wel.Ch.	8	—	
Santa Cruz	109,142			Nil	..	—	—	
Tierra del Fuego ..	8,299			Nil	..	—	—	
Los Andes	34,740			Nil	..	—	—	
	527,917	491,572	.93	9 Stations	7 Missions	22	5	
Grand Totals	1,153,119	10,348,189	8.97	75 Stations	42 Missions	454	326	100,000†

* The figures in these columns denote the total number of workers (not including wives) in each Territory.

† Only a personal estimate can be made of the Protestant community.

PARAGUAY.

SUMMARY.

Oriental :

Area	61,647 square miles.
Population	853,321.

Occidental :

Area	100,000 square miles.
Population	50,000.

Density	5 per square mile.
Principal Mission Stations	10.
Missions and Societies ..	13.
Foreign Workers	37 (not including wives).
National Workers ..	20 (not including wives).
Protestant Community ..	Possibly 4,000, including all foreigners who are Protestant.

PARAGUAY.

The Principal Non-Roman Catholic Organizations.

1. The Anglican Church (A.Ch.).
2. Christian Missions in Many Lands (C.M.M.L.).
3. The Disciples of Christ, or United Christian Missionary Society (U.C.M.S.).
4. The German Evangelical Church (G.Ev.Ch.).
5. South American Missionary Society (S.A.M.S.).
6. Inland South America Missionary Union (I.S.A.M.U.).
7. Southern Baptist Convention (S.B.C.).
8. The Salvation Army (S.A.).
9. The Seventh-Day Adventists (S.D.A.).
10. The American Bible Society (A.B.S.).
11. The British and Foreign Bible Society (B.F.B.S.).
12. Independent Worker (Ind.).
13. The Samaritan Missionary Association (S.M.A.).

PARAGUAY.

Districts.	Area.	Population.	Density.	Principal Mission Stations.	Missions.	Foreign Workers.*	National Workers.*	Protestant Community.
Occidental Section	100,000	50,000 (Estimate)	.5	Makthlaway	S.A.M.S.	4	3	
				Nanawa	S.A.M.S.	4	3	
				Chaco	S.M.A.	2	—	
Oriental Section	61,647	853,321	13.8					
Asunción ..		93,000		Asunción	S.D.A.	2	2	
					S.A.	2	2	
					S.B.C.	1	1	
					A.Ch.	1	—	
					G.Ev.Ch.	1	—	
					A.B.S.	—	—	
					B.F.B.S.	—	—	
					C.M.M.L.	3	—	
					U.C.M.S.	6	—	
Concepción		15,000		Concepción	I.S.A.M.U.	2	1	
				Belén	Ind.	1	1	
Encarnación		12,500		Encarnación	I.S.A.M.U.	2	2	
Paraguarí		10,000		Paraguarí	I.S.A.M.U.	1	1	
Villa Rica		26,000		Villa Rica	I.S.A.M.U.	2	2	
					S.A.	2	1	
San Pedro		8,700		Nil	..	—	—	
Villa del Pilar		10,000		,,	..	—	—	
Caraguatay				,,	..	—	—	
Yhu ..				,,	..	—	—	
Caazapá ..		678,121		Yegros	I.S.A.M.U.	1	1	
San Ygnacio				Nil	..	—	—	
Quiindy ..				,,	..	—	—	
Villeta ..				,,	..	—	—	
	161,647	903,321	5	10 Stations	13 Missions	37	20	4,000

* Not including wives.

URUGUAY.

SUMMARY.

Area	72,153 square miles.
Population	1,720,468.
Density	23.84 per square mile.
Principal Mission Stations	10.
Missions and Societies ..	15.
Foreign Workers	36 (not including wives).
National Workers ..	39 (not including wives).
Protestant Community ..	Probably 15,000, including Protestant foreigners and the large Waldensian colony.

URUGUAY.

The Principal Non-Roman Catholic Organizations.

1. The Anglican Church (A.Ch.).
2. Christian Missions in Many Lands (C.M.M.L.).
3. The German Evangelical Church (G.Ev.Ch.).
4. The Methodist Episcopal Church (M.E.F.B.).
5. Southern Baptist Convention (S.B.C.).
6. The Salvation Army (S.A.).
7. The Seventh-Day Adventists (S.D.A.).
8. The Scots Presbyterian Church (S.P.Ch.).
9. The American Bible Society (A.B.S.).
10. The British and Foreign Bible Society (B.F.B.S.).
11. The Pentecostal Church (Pen.Ch.).
12. Women's Christian Temperance Union (W.C.T.U.).
13. The Young Men's Christian Association (Y.M.C.A.).
14. The Young Women's Christian Association (Y.W.C.A.).
15. The Waldensian Church (W.Ch.).

URUGUAY.

Departments.	Area.	Population.	Density.	Principal Mission Stations.	Missions.	Foreign Workers.*	National Workers.*	Protestant Community.
Artigas ..	4,394	42,624	9.70	Nil	..	—	—	
Canelones	1,834	158,977	86.68	Las Piedras	C.M.M.L.	1	—	
				Canelones	C.M.M.L.	1	—	
Cerro-Largo	5,763	75,260	13.06	Nil				
Colonia ..	2,193	99,993	45.60	Colonia				
				Valdense	W.Ch.	1	6	
				Colonia S.				
				Pedro	S.D.A.	1	1	
Durazno ..	5,525	72,795	13.18	Durazno	M.E.F.B.	—	1	
Flores ..	1,744	27,436	15.73	Nil	..	—	—	
Florida ..	4,673	83,108	17.78	,,	..	—	—	
Maldonado	1,587	51,516	32.46	,,	..	—	—	
Minas ..	4,819	91,387	18.96	Minas	S.B.C.	1	—	
Montevideo	256	439,129	1715.35	Montevideo	S.B.C.	2	1	
				,,	C.M.M.L.	—	—	
				,,	M.E.F.B.	8	6	
				,,	S.A.	4	6	
				,,	S.D.A.	2	2	
				,,	Y.M.C.A.	6	6	
				,,	Y.W.C.A.	2	2	
				,,	A.Ch.	1	—	
				,,	G.Ev.Ch.	1	—	
				,,	S.P.Ch	—	—	
				,,	A.B.S.	—	—	
				,,	B.F.B.S.	—	—	
				,,	Pen.Ch.	—	1	
				,,	W.C.T.U.	—	1	
Paysandú	5,115	63,891	12.49	Paysandú	S.A.	1	2	
					S.B.C.	1	—	
					S.D.A.	1	2	
Rio Negro	3,269	35,778	10.94	Nil	..	—	—	
Rivera ..	3,793	57,853	15.25	,,	..	—	—	
Rocha ..	4,280	62,421	14.58	,,	..	—	—	
Salto ..	4,865	76,690	15.76	Salto	S.A.	1	2	
San José ..	2,688	79,305	29.50	San José	C.M.M.L.	1	—	
Soriano ..	3,561	69,277	19.45	Nil	..	—	—	
Tacuarembó	8,112	80,192	9.89	,,	..	—	—	
Treinta y Tres	3,682	52,836	14.35	,,	..	—	—	
	72,153	1,720,468	23.84	10 Stations	15 Missions	36	39	15,000

* Not including wives.

APPENDIX B.

EVANGELICAL SCHOOLS.

Country.	Town.	Mission.	Kindergarten.	Primary.	Secondary.	Total Pupils.	Foreign Teachers.	National Teachers.
Argentina	Buenos Aires	Union*	1	1	1	300	6	23
	,, ,,	U.L.C.	1	1	1	500	4	20
	,, ,,	S.B.C.	—	1	—	80	2	5
	Rosario	M.E.F.B.	1	1	—	150	4	10
	,,	,,	1	1	—	150	1	5
	,,	Union†	—	1	—	150	5	5
	Godoy Cruz	S.B.C.	—	1	—	80	1	3
	San Julián	A.Ch.	—	1	—	25	1	1
	Trelew	,,	—	1	—	50	2	1
	Junín	,,	—	1	—	50	1	1
	Embarcación	,,	—	1	—	10	1	1
	Various	M.Ch.	—	4	—	150	1	4
	,,	M.E.F.B.	—	10	—	500	—	20
	,,	S.D.A.	—	16	1	942	9	22
Paraguay ..	Asunción	U.C.M.S.	1	1	1	150	8	13
	Villa Rica	I.S.A.M.U.	—	1	—	9	1	—
	Sapucay	A.Ch.	—	1	—	—	—	—
	Chaco	S.A.M.S.	—	1	—	20	2	1
	Belén	Ind.‡	—	1	—	20	1	1
	Trinidad	S.D.A.	—	1	—	40	—	1
Uruguay ..	Montevideo	M.E.F.B.	1	1	1	400	10	18
	,, ,,		—	1	—	85	2	6
	Various	S.D.A.	—	3	—	100	—	3
			6	52	5	3,961	62	164

* Disciples of Christ and Methodist Episcopals.
† Anglicans and Methodists.
‡ Dr. Lindsay.

N.B.—In the above list only those schools have been listed whose purpose is distinctly Christian and which are under the auspices of some religious group, either racial or missionary in its purpose. For this reason the " Argentine Philanthropic Schools and Institutes," under the direction of the Rev. W. C. Morris, of the S.A.M.S., are omitted, since they work under a local Board which is non-sectarian. They are educating, under Christian influences, over six thousand children, in primary grades, and should be taken into account in estimating such schools in the Argentine Republic.

There are also a number of British schools, under directly religious influences, but working independently. Hence, they cannot be included. Yet they all contribute largely to the sum of Christian education that is being given in the area. It is reported that there are twenty-one such schools in or around Buenos Aires, and three in the provinces. There are two in Montevideo. The total number of pupils exceeds 2,500, and there are about two hundred on the teaching staffs, including some fifty who are nationals teaching subjects in Spanish. Most of the headmasters and headmistresses are graduates of British universities, or hold Board of Education certificates. The nationals are generally normal graduates.

I*

APPENDIX C.

THEOLOGICAL SEMINARIES.

Country.	Control.	Students.	Professors.	Length of Course.	Location.
Argentina ..	Union*	5	5	3 years	Buenos Aires
	S.B.C.	10	6	,,	,, ,,
		15	11		

BIBLE INSTITUTES.

Country.	Control.	Students.	Professors.	Length of Course.	Location.
Argentina ..	C.N.	12	3		Buenos Aires
	Union†	12	4		Azul
	Union‡	15	8	3 years	Buenos Aires
Paraguay ..	I.S.A.M.U.	20	2		Villarica
		59	17		

* Disciples of Christ, Methodist Episcopals and Waldensians. The last named have students, but no professor, in the Seminary. The others provide professors, building, etc., as a joint venture in co-operation.

† The Christian and Missionary Alliance and the Evangelical Union of South America. Azul is a town in the southern part of the Province of Buenos Aires.

‡ Disciples of Christ and Methodist Episcopals. This is an institute for women workers, the only one of its kind in the area, perhaps in South America.

N.B.—There are probably a few other small groups of students of this class, as for the training of workers among the Indians in the Chaco, but statistics are not available.

The racial groups continue to count on receiving their ministers and pastors from the various home lands, although most of their young people speak Spanish, and the time cannot be far distant when native-born ministers will become a necessity if the people are to be held to the evangelical faith.

The Union Seminary is the only institution in the area that, as a preparation for theological study, demands the completion of the national secondary course of study, or its equivalent. It is also the only one that makes such a demand in all South America outside of the Republic of Brazil.

Special mention must be made of the " Technical Institute " of the Young Men's Christian Association, in Montevideo, the training school for national secretaries of the Association. The course consists of four years, but the first two are given in local associations, in Mexico, Chile, Perú, Buenos Aires and Rio de Janeiro. All students come together in Montevideo for the final two years. The course is intensive and the entrance requirements are rigid and high. As a consequence a very fine group of young men are being prepared for the work of the Association in Latin America. There are fourteen students under eight professors.

APPENDIX D.

THE PRINCIPAL NON-ROMAN CATHOLIC GROUPS.

Church or Group.	Members.	Churches.	Sunday Schools.	Halls.	Hospitals.	Orphanages.	Pastors Lay Preachers.	Students.	Date Begun.
A.Ch. ..	—	15	11	7	—	3	22	—	1825
S.P.Ch. ..	900	7	18	6	—	—	12	—	1829
M.E.F.B.	5,846	55	123	—	—	1	73	3	1836
G.Ev.Ch...	12,000	25	30	5	—	—	18	—	1843
W.Ch. ..	3,500	18	40	6	—	—	8	2	1857
S.A. ..	2,332	45	47	—	1	1	162	—	1890
S.D.A. ..	2,400	50	70	—	1	—	40	—	1897
E.U.S.A.	400	13	22	9	—	—	12	6	1898
C.M.A. ..	258	16	16	2	—	—	10	6	1900
D.R.Ch. ..	450	4	6	—	—	—	1	—	1900
F.B. ..	3,000	40	40	—	—	—	10	—	—
S.B.C. ..	2,980	49	89	—	—	—	40	10	1903
U.C.M.S.	126	3	4	1	—	—	4	—	1906
C.M.M.L.	210	7	12	2	—	—	9	—	1909
Ind. ..	15	1	2	10	—	—	1	—	1915
U.L.C. ..	495	8	8	—	—	—	3	—	1918
M.Ch. ..	205	8	10	5	—	—	8	—	1919
C.N. ..	80	3	4	2	—	—	3	12	1920
Ap.Ch. ..	25	2	1	—	—	—	3	—	1922
Ar.Ch. ..	60	1	2	5	—	—	1	—	1923
E.C.Ch. ..	35	2	2	—	—	—	2	—	1923
D.Ch. ..	250	1	1	—	—	—	1	—	1924
	35,567	373	558	60	2	5	443	39	

The above list is incomplete, since some groups do not give statistics. It is interesting to note that by subtracting the racial groups and adding two thousand for possible omissions, there remain about twenty thousand as the net membership of the strictly Evangelical Churches. Some groups, as the German Evangelical, obviously report community members only.

APPENDIX E.

Note on Occupation

Argentina.

The federal district of Buenos Aires, whose area is about seventy square miles, has almost two million inhabitants. According to some of the most recent calculations, the figure would even exceed two millions, and the number is rapidly growing. Within this district there are at least thirty different non-Roman Catholic Christian organizations at work, with a total of some two hundred and fifty workers, not including wives, but including both foreign and native-born men. While no exact statement can be made as to the Reformed Christian community, yet, including foreigners such as British and German residents, it is probable that it may number around forty-five thousand persons.

The Province of Buenos Aires, which includes the federal district, is by far the most fully occupied section of the Republic, as regards evangelical workers, there being at least thirty-five preaching stations, outside the city of Buenos Aires, which represent the work of as many different organizations. In the whole Province, according to the most careful study available, there are three hundred and forty workers, not counting wives, and the evangelical community may be estimated at fifty thousand.

When we come to the other provinces and territories, however, we find a very different situation. Eight of these are completely unoccupied. In this vast region of almost four hundred and twenty thousand square miles there is a population of nearly three hundred thousand, with not a single native worker, and yet with a population that is almost wholly of Spanish speech and Argentine by birth.

The occupation of the remaining provinces and territories may be given as follows : Santa Fé, with a population of 1,214,571, has eighteen foreign and eighteen national workers, very largely centralized in the capital city and one other city ; Córdoba, with almost a million population, has twenty-one workers in some eight centres ; Entre Rios, with over half a million, has fifty-nine workers in seven principal centres, with outlying work in the rural region ; Corrientes, with over four hundred thousand people, has fifteen workers ; Santiago del Estero, with 350,816 inhabitants, has two workers, both foreigners ; Tucumán, with over four hundred thousand inhabitants, has five workers, four of them foreigners ; San Luis, with 149,722 people, has two workers, both nationals ; Mendoza, with nearly four hundred thousand people, has six native workers and two foreigners ; San Juan, with 156,433 people, has only two native workers ; Catamarca, with 120,422 inhabitants, has one worker, a foreigner ; Salta, with a population of more than a hundred and fifty thousand, has nine workers, eight of them foreigners, and all engaged in work among the Indian tribes of the Chaco ; Jujuy, among more than eighty-five thousand, has three workers, all foreigners ; Misiones, in which one of the strong Missions has its headquarters, with a population around seventy thousand, has thirteen workers, eleven of them foreigners ; and La Pampa, with more than a hundred and forty thousand population, has six workers, three of them foreigners. Chubut, with a considerable foreign population among its more than thirty thousand inhabitants, is occupied only by foreigners—the Welsh who have work in 16 de Octubre and Bryn Crwn, and the Dutch Reformed colony from South Africa, whose work centres in Comodoro Rivadavia.

One has only to read these facts and to study the map in order to realize the state of occupation of this Republic, the most important and that which has most promise for the future of all the Latin American republics. Evangelical Christianity has so far merely touched the fringe of the problem. With its forces very largely centred in the Province of Buenos Aires, the great hinterland remains practically untouched. The Roman Catholic forces, too, are very largely centred in Buenos Aires, so that the inhabitants of the great interior may well cry out with David: " No man cared for my soul ! "

Paraguay.

In Paraguay proper, lying between the two great rivers, the Paraguay and the Upper Paraná, six out of the thirteen administrative districts are occupied in part by thirteen Missions in ten stations with a total of fifty-seven workers, twenty of them nationals. The population of the occupied areas is about two hundred thousand, while that of the unoccupied districts is around seven hundred thousand. Thus, nearly three-quarters of the population is unreached by any evangelical body. Moreover, of the eighty-four Roman Catholic priests said to be in Paraguay, half are in the capital city, Asunción, leaving the remaining eight hundred thousand people, scattered over a territory of over a hundred and sixty thousand square miles, to be ministered to by forty men who lack all modern means of communication and must reach the people, if they reach them at all, over country roads that are often impassable and never offer easy travel.

Beyond the Paraguay river, in the disputed territory of the Chaco, where there is an estimated population of fifty thousand wild Indians, we have a huge area of about a hundred thousand square miles with only three mission stations. Two of these belong to the South American Missionary Society, with fourteen workers, and one to the Samaritan Missionary Association, with two foreign workers. The country is but sparsely settled and the work is thus made most difficult. This great inland Republic, the Mesopotamia of South America, with great natural resources to be developed and a people peculiarly susceptible to an intelligent approach by Christian workers, is only just beginning to learn of the Gospel message and to be put in possession of the Bible.

Uruguay.

There are fifteen Missions and other organizations at work in this little Republic, among a population of more than a million and a half. This is the only Republic in South America that has no Indian population, and hence no Indian problem, and the work is among a thoroughly homogeneous and kindly disposed people. The means of communication are much superior to those in Paraguay, since there are fairly good country roads, and a number of railways, largely British in their ownership, traverse the most thickly settled parts of the Republic. Yet the evangelical work centres very largely in the capital city, Montevideo, which contains also more than a quarter of the entire population of the country. In this city there are probably some fifty of the total number of seventy-five evangelical workers located in the country, many of them in school work, in the Christian Associations, and engaged in looking after the spiritual welfare of the foreign colonies. Some of the evangelical groups, such as the Methodists, the Southern Baptists, and the Salvation Army, have out-stations in some of the towns of the interior, which are visited from time to time, or are looked after in general by national workers. Yet, as in both Argentina and Paraguay, the rural districts are woefully neglected and are practically outside of the sound of the Gospel.

Conclusion.

Perhaps a few words more in regard to the importance of this region as a strategic centre from which to exercise evangelical influence throughout the continent may not be amiss. According to the latest statistics available, the population of the three Republics which enter into this study is around thirteen million.

That of Buenos Aires alone, the principal city, is about two million. The arc of a circle of four hundred miles, struck with this city as a base, takes in one-third of the Republic and one-fourth of its population, and also extends over into the neighbouring Republic of Uruguay. In this area the population is comparatively compact, the ratio being eight inhabitants to the square kilometre. Outside, in the country districts, the ratio is one inhabitant per square kilometre. This indicates the importance of Buenos Aires, not only to Argentina but also to Paraguay and Uruguay. But if, within the radius of the circle already described, we make another which takes in the city and suburbs of Buenos Aires, we would find that within it would fall one-fifth of the entire number of inhabitants of the Republic. That is to say, the opulent city of Buenos Aires not only draws its revenues from the provinces, but directs the entire Republic, since it is the federal capital and the seat of the elaborate federal Government.

Moreover, it has been pointed out by authoritative figures that the economic capacity of Argentina, tested by any of the ordinary tests, is equal to the capacity of all the rest of the South American republics bulked together. In other words, the ten million inhabitants of Argentina produce and consume more than the fifty-five millions of the other republics of South America. Of the area of South America only sixteen per cent. is Argentine territory, yet this fragment is economically of greater importance than all the rest of the continent. In another seventy years it is claimed that the population of Buenos Aires will be eight millions, and this ought to mean that the Republic as a whole will have a population of one hundred million.

But this is not only an economic centre, for Buenos Aires is also the cultural centre of South America, if not also of all Latin America. Its intellectual output exceeds that of any other city of Latin America, and only one who lives within its limits can appreciate the tremendous cultural activities which are being

carried on. As Buenos Aires goes, and as Argentina
goes, economically, intellectually, spiritually, so will
all Latin America go. Therefore, no Mission organization can make a mistake in strengthening and furthering
its work in this great teeming city, with its heaving
tides of modern civilization, and in the great hinterland
of Argentina, Paraguay and Uruguay, from which it
draws its physical support and to which it stands as
Athens stood to ancient Greece, or Paris—the only
rival of Buenos Aires among Latin cities—stands to
modern France.

These facts will also serve to explain in part the
strategy of the various evangelical organizations that
have centred their work so largely in the Province of
Buenos Aires and in the federal district. The strategic
importance of the three capital cities of these Republics
is in a peculiar way unique even in the South American
continent. Nevertheless, while the adequate occupation
of these centres is of the first importance, the attention
of Protestant Missions should be more and more
turned to the great rural areas. " This ye ought to have
done, and not left the other undone."

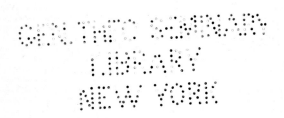

The Survey Series

The WORLD DOMINION SURVEY SERIES attempts to describe briefly and clearly the situation in various countries as viewed from the standpoint of the Kingdom of God.

INSULINDE : A brief Survey of the Dutch East Indies. With Map.
Price 6d. (post paid, 7d.)

A BIRD'S-EYE VIEW OF LATIN AMERICA. With Map.
Price 6d. (post paid, 7d.)

THE TASK OF THE CHRISTIAN CHURCH : A World Survey. Edited by Thomas Cochrane. Price 7/6 (post paid, 8/-)
"A book which should be in the hands of missionaries, ministers, Church secretaries, Sunday School superintendents—in fact, anyone who holds any position of leadership in Christian work, whether at home or abroad."
British Weekly.

THE LAND OF THE VANISHED CHURCH : A Survey of North Africa. By J. J. Cooksey. With Map. Price 2/- (post paid, 2/3)
"The book is one of great, almost fascinating interest ; it is wonderful how much information is crowded into its 100 odd pages."—*Missionary Review of All Nations.*

A GREAT EMANCIPATION : A Survey of Nyasaland. By W. J. W. Roome. Price 1/- (post paid, 1/2). With Map, 4/- (post paid, 4/3)
"The facts . . . brought together in this masterly statement deal with the land and its history, the people, the growth of the African Church, the missions in Nyasaland, the progress of Islam, education and the place of the Bible."—*Life of Faith.*

NIGERIA : The Land, the People, and Christian Progress. By J. Lowry Maxwell. With Maps. Stiff paper cover, 3/6 (post paid, 3/9)
Cloth boards, gilt lettered, 5/- (post paid, 5/6)
"Gives a bird's-eye view of the conditions in Nigeria from the Christian standpoint. . . . A picturesquely told story, giving a more vivid view of these things than a more elaborate and detailed description."—*U. F. S. Record.*

AN EASTERN PALIMPSEST : A brief Survey of Turkey, Syria, Palestine and Egypt. By O. Wyon. With Maps. Stiff paper cover, 2/6 (post paid, 2/9)
"Attractively written . . . full of useful information."—*Bible in the World.*

LIGHT AND DARKNESS IN EAST AFRICA : A Survey of A. E. Sudan, Uganda, Abyssinia, Eritrea and the Somalilands. With Maps. Cloth boards, gilt lettered, 5/- (post paid, 5/6). Stiff paper cover, 3/6 (post paid, 3/10)
"The World Dominion Survey Series, to which this book belongs, gains immensely in its impressiveness and usefulness as it proceeds with its accounts of the influence of Christianity throughout the world."—*Times Literary Supplement.*

THE LOWLAND INDIANS OF AMAZONIA. By K. G. Grubb. With 14 Maps. Cloth boards, gilt lettered, 5/- (post paid, 5/6)
"The writer has travelled extensively in the Amazon Valley, and has acquired a very intimate knowledge of the habits and temperament of the Lowland Indians, which makes his book very interesting to all those concerned in the problems presented by those very difficult races."—*South American Journal.*

CHURCH AND MISSIONS IN MANCHURIA : A Survey of a Strategic Field. By Alexander R. Mackenzie. With Maps. Stiff paper cover, 2/6 (post paid, 2/9)

THE WAY OF THE WHITE FIELDS IN RHODESIA : A Survey of Christian Enterprise in Northern and Southern Rhodesia. By Edwin W. Smith. With Maps. Cloth boards, gilt lettered, 5/- (post paid, 5/6)

OTHERS WILL FOLLOW

WORLD DOMINION PRESS, 1, Tudor Street, London, E.C.4